The Path to Conscious Leadership

The Path to Conscious Leadership

Five Steps to Better Decisions and Results

Seema Dhanoa

BARLOW BOOKS

Copyright © Seema Dhanoa, 2025

All rights reserved, including those for data and text mining, AI training, and similar technologies. No part of this publication may be reproduced, stored in a retrieval system or transmitted, in any form or by any means, without prior written consent of the publisher.

Library and Archives Canada Cataloguing in Publication data available upon request.

ISBN: 978-1-998841-20-2

Printed in Canada

Publisher: Sarah Scott
Book producer: Tracy Bordian/At Large Editorial Services
Cover design: Paul Hodgson
Interior design and layout: Ruth Dwight

For more information, visit www.barlowbooks.com

Barlow Book Publishing Inc.
96 Elm Avenue, Toronto, ON
M4W 1P2 Canada

*For my family and dearest friends,
Thank you for always standing by my side
and believing in me.*

Contents

Introduction	ix
Understanding the Error-Prone Mind	1
Step 1: Be Present	31
Step 2: Become Heart-Centred	61
Step 3: Stay Interconnected	87
Step 4: Feel the Future	109
Step 5: Think with Abundance	131
Leading Conscious Transformation	153
Conclusion	181
Bibliography	189
Index	205
About the Author	212

Introduction

It's this century's biggest challenge: In a time of unprecedented change that requires all of our attention, we are paying less attention than ever before. We experience everyday life from within our own bubbles. On public transit, in the cocoon of our cars, on elevators, or walking down the street, we interact with our devices more than we do with other people.

Work life is no different. Not long ago I walked into a client meeting with my laptop, smartphone, a notebook, and pen. I settled into my seat and looked at the other ten participants in the room. Everyone had their laptop open while the screen at the front of the room displayed our agenda. The meeting started, and I found myself glancing at both the screen and my laptop. One of the participants hadn't silenced her phone, and the intermittent "dings" irritated me. I found myself constantly thinking, *Why doesn't she silence her phone?* By now I was struggling to keep up with the discussion. And when I looked around the room I saw the others working on their laptops. Clearly they, too, were not on top of the conversation. The hour-and-a-half-long meeting felt like an energy-draining slog.

As business leaders, we have so many tools to aid our productivity that we end up trying to do too much at once and, as a result, are unable to focus on anything. Yet the world is full of urgent issues that need our attention—issues that could hurt our businesses if we lose focus. The landscape is volatile, uncertain, complex, and ambiguous (VUCA, as the U.S. military calls it). It's cluttered with economic woes, political turmoil, and geopolitical tensions. And then there is the monumental challenge of climate change. How we respond to that particular challenge—as individuals and as business leaders—is absolutely crucial. If Earth breaches global warming targets, humanity will be on a path of peril.

And what about the as-yet-unregulated world of artificial intelligence? Software that aims to mimic human intelligence and problem-solving as it performs tasks and creates content—audio, code, images, text, videos, and simulations—is revolutionizing how we live and work. The next iteration of the Internet will also cause a big shift. Centralized platforms and services could move to more decentralized networks and protocols, and a host of newer technologies will fuel that evolution. Intelligent data will enable seamless interaction across systems, people, and devices. It won't be long before billions of devices are connected worldwide. That global hyper-connection could create a new form of collective human consciousness. Only time will tell what all of this will ultimately mean.

So how do we lead in this VUCA world? Unfortunately, the management techniques developed over the past century just aren't cutting it anymore. For a long time, our external environment was predictable. Economists, business leaders, and other professionals got used to valuing certainty and stability. Companies built out their infrastructure and machinery for efficiency and scale. Foreshadowed by beliefs and practices from the Industrial era, these methods became the norm. Leaders adopted frameworks and tools—all the mechanics they needed to manage performance and profits. Organizations hummed along this way for many years. But things are now starting to fray. Cracks have appeared and are expanding. The external environment is no longer predictable. The beliefs and assumptions of the past do not hold true today because our context has changed. Leaders accustomed to following their recipes for success are finding it challenging to maintain results.

All of this poses a serious dilemma for today's leaders. Addressing the problems of this century and preparing for the future requires broad thinking across several issues. We need to be ready to meet our many challenges simultaneously and with flexibility. Changes in our organizations must reflect the pace of our external environment, and it needs to happen despite everything else that requires our attention.

It's tempting to shy away from the challenges and just stay the course—that's a lot less stressful than creating significant change. It's also easier to blame an inability to transform on lack of capacity. But if you do nothing and simply maintain the status quo, you open up your organization to errors and significant risks. These could be due to self-inflicted wounds or external issues. If you don't pay attention to the changing world then you will get disrupted—either forced to pivot or rendered obsolete. Blockbuster, the chain of video and DVD rental stores, had a chance to buy Netflix for $50 million. But they viewed the dot-com revolution as overblown, and believed that online business wasn't sustainable and would never make money. They got that one totally wrong and paid the price: They went bankrupt, and the final few Blockbuster stores closed in 2014.

Getting caught in the VUCA world without a clear understanding of reality leads to bad decisions. Business leaders must take the blinders off and pay close attention to what's happening under their watch. Volkswagen barely survived its emissions scandal of 2015, when it was forced to admit equipping 11 million cars worldwide with a device that would alter emissions test results to show compliance with environmental regulations. What had allowed the deception to continue for years was corruption, to be sure, but it was also due to a company culture that tolerated internal rule-breaking. The company had failed to adequately oversee the activities of its engine development department, and then-CEO Martin Winterkorn didn't respond to indications the company was using illegal diesel engine technology. It cost Volkswagen billions, and its new leadership has since put in place a reformed compliance culture and an expanded whistleblower program.

My intent for writing this book is to help you avoid the abyss by becoming conscious leaders—that is, by using your head, your heart, and your gut to see the world around you *as it actually is*. Conscious leadership will put you in a position to make better decisions and steer your organization into the future.

Learning this new way of being and thinking will challenge you. You'll need to retrain your brain so that you can avoid business blunders when threats are in plain view. You'll have to eliminate biases, assumptions, and false narratives leading to mental errors that conceal the fast-changing reality around you. And you will need to quiet the chatter inside your mind so that you can see, hear, and feel the fast-changing reality around you. Only then can you begin to imagine innovative ways to handle the substantial challenges that technology, climate change, and so many other factors create for your business.

> *The world that you see comes to life by what you perceive and how you pay attention.*

Conscious leadership will help you lead with clarity and purpose, instead of just meeting quarterly targets. The greatest leadership quest of the 21st century is the chance to reimagine the future. Finding a path that reduces harm and adds greater value requires a new form of leadership. Today's leaders need to have a high level of awareness of how their thoughts, beliefs, and actions manifest into outcomes. This knowing will help leaders to expand perspectives, drive stronger results, and change the world for the better.

The concept of *consciousness* is mysterious and has been since the great ancient philosophers sought to explain it millennia ago: a deep awareness of our heart and our thoughts that evolves our being. As a modern buzzword, however, "consciousness" is often misused and confused with mindfulness—conscious eating, conscious habits, conscious shopping, and even conscious uncoupling. The same kind of confusion exists around the term *conscious leadership*. For example, while authenticity and empathy are good qualities in a leader, they don't constitute conscious leadership. Too often, they're simply good management practices. In another example, I once came across a "conscious leadership" conference that was actually about environmental sustainability. Yes, caring for the planet is a conscious practice, but it's not conscious leadership.

It's not surprising that many leaders don't even know about conscious leadership. Business schools and organizations don't teach it. Here is how I define it:

Conscious leadership is leading with awareness by being present and aligning thoughts, emotions, intuition, and the body to perceive the moment-to-moment experience.

My hope is that after reading this book, you will begin to think in new ways, ways that come from a deeper understanding of your inner state and the outer world. You'll appreciate that when you lead with consciousness it has a direct and positive influence on outcomes, that leading change to a brighter future comes from intention and noticing interconnectedness, that paying attention to your heart and intuition enhances your capacity to perceive and influence your responses, and that inspiration for the future comes from thinking with a perspective of limitless potential and possibilities.

I begin the book by discussing how the brain uses shortcuts that can cause mental errors, and how you can identify and overcome those. Then, I'll walk you through the five steps to becoming a conscious leader and how to create conscious transformation in your organization. These five steps, summarized below, will help you to increase your awareness and understanding of reality.

THE FIVE STEPS TO CONSCIOUS LEADERSHIP

Step 1: Be Present

We miss things when we fail to process the information around us. This is common because we are surrounded by so many distractions, and the brain has limits. So we let our mind drift to random thoughts instead of focusing on the reality that's happening in front of us. We'll misread an email or not hear what someone says. Mistakes then happen. But when we're present, our attention is focused. We free the mind from clutter, wandering thoughts, and attachments to ideas. This allows insights to emerge from what is actually happening. Our attention is a precious resource, and we need to be aware of how we use it—and when we let it go.

Step 2: Become Heart-centred

Imagine you're discussing a new innovation with your colleagues, and you feel excitement in the room. You're about to make a big decision, and what happens? You also hear a voice coming from somewhere deep inside of you. You get a really strong feeling about what to do. This is the conscious experience. The heart can sense, feel, and send messages to the brain. Intuition can physically manifest sensations in the body.

Too often, a lot of mental chatter fills our minds. When we can clear that chatter, we hear our heart and intuition, and align our thoughts. We can appreciate the heart's capacity and how feelings work with cognition, and this connection helps with thinking and decision-making. Gut feelings represent something critical, and learning how to listen deeply to our inner voice enables a greater capacity to perceive, understand, and connect with others. Heart-centred practices generate new perspectives and thinking to discover opportunities and innovation. Learning to read and interpret the signals from the heart and gut will help you to home in on this intelligence.

Step 3: Stay Interconnected

Many of us are under what I call an illusion of separateness: a disconnect between ourselves and others that means we see only a fraction of what's happening. Mastering techniques of interconnectedness helps us to understand the relationship between ourselves and the world. It helps us to recognize the beliefs and assumptions that reinforce separateness and linear thinking. Seeking the opinions of others is a crucial step. Because most of us don't notice everything that's happening around us, hearing other opinions provides insight into what we might be missing.

By mastering this skill, you'll learn more about your stakeholders. You will be better able to perceive the many relationships that intersect with your organization and require your attention. You'll also be able to see the hidden beliefs that can block new ideas. That will lead to better decisions.

Step 4: Feel the Future

In every moment, the brain predicts what will happen next based on the information stored in its long-term memory. Let's say you were dropped into a technology project tomorrow. If you've worked on a few such projects in the past, you have the experience that tells you what to expect, and you'll have no problem handling it. But if it's your first time working on such a project, you are likely to struggle because you don't have the memories in your brain to help you predict how the work will unfold. It leads to mental stress and fear-related behaviours that impact cognition and decision-making. That's why we must learn to envision the future like it's happening now. We need to imagine it with details so that our brains can do better predicting and thinking about the future. It's tempting to think that means we should set goals; after all, goals appeal to the rational nature of the brain. But it's just as important to *feel the future*: to consciously set intention. This shifts your focus to what you will experience through actions. Goals are about doing; intentions are about being. We need to think about both.

Step 5: Think with Abundance

People with an abundance mindset have a positive attitude despite the challenges that come their way. In J.R.R. Tolkien's *Lord of The*

Rings, Sam Gamgee, Frodo's best friend and companion on his quest to destroy the ring of power, never lets go of his abundance mindset. Despite being low on food, water, and other supplies, and facing the armies of Mordor, Sam meets every challenge as an opportunity to succeed. His outlook to achieve the mission does not get constrained by thoughts of depleted resources. Thinking with abundance focuses on limitless potential, despite your resources. You imagine new ways of doing things to achieve more—without getting bogged down by what you don't have.

Leaders who switch their thinking to an abundance mindset can see beyond the existing market, and maybe consider expanding it. Uber Eats did that when they expanded into grocery delivery. Leaders with an abundance mindset could even develop a new market space, like what happened with the smart home—goodbye traditional thermostat, hello intelligent devices. Abundance thinking gives leaders willingness to accept risks because they don't fear what they have to lose, but focus on what they have to gain.

The opposite is the scarcity mindset, when you focus on what you lack. Business leaders routinely fall into scarcity thinking. They can't see past their market share and their competitive set, and focus mainly on increasing their piece of that finite pie. By staying stuck in market boundaries, they're missing the opportunity to innovate and find new opportunities.

Mastering the skills of conscious leadership is essential for those who truly want to transform organizations. Corporate transformation is difficult. Implementing wholesale change to reach aspirations, and running a business at the same time, overwhelms people's capacity to function. So many corporate transformation strategies fall short of innovation or creating real change. Companies fall into a pattern of doing what they already do, and underlying beliefs and assumptions go unchallenged. Transforming a culture means shifting mindsets. It also means you need to build a conscious culture, using conscious innovation and diving into immersive experiences. Mastering the five steps in this book will help you do that. It will transform you into a conscious leader able to lead your organization through the complexity and challenges of this century toward a brighter future.

I hope you find inspiration through the words in this book and see a new path forward. Take your time reading the following chapters to absorb the content and reflect. Give yourself space to integrate what you learn. The more you understand yourself, the greater your ability to use conscious experience. Self-awareness intrinsically links with external awareness and enhances how we comprehend reality.

When we evolve our thoughts and our being, we change our reality. That reality is a new world that we can see and act upon.

Understanding the Error-Prone Mind

We think we understand reality. We feel certain that we know what's going on in the moment. It's right there in front of us, isn't it? But an experiment conducted 25 years ago by psychologist Daniel Simons and his student Christopher Chabris shows that we are in fact missing reality. In the experiment, a group of participants watched a video of people passing a basketball around. One team was wearing white and the other team was wearing black. The participants were told to count the number of times the team wearing white passed the ball, while ignoring the team wearing black. At some point during this game, a person dressed as a gorilla walked into the middle of the action for nine seconds, thumped its chest and walked away. You'd think the participants would have noticed the gorilla. Yet, half of them later said *they did not see it*. The gorilla was invisible to them.

The "invisible gorilla" experiment revealed some important things. We miss a lot of what's actually happening, and we have no idea that we are missing it. It also shows that we come to expect what we think we will see. And that we don't notice something in familiar settings because we assume we know what's there.

The mind has strong convictions. We don't doubt or question what we see. Our vision and senses pull in information to help us understand reality. The brain interprets what's happening. But along the way, we can end up making mental errors. Sometimes it's silly mistakes like grabbing the wrong ingredient from the kitchen cupboard, or putting the cereal box instead of the milk into the fridge. At other times, we can forget to do a task. Once, while I was meeting with a friend after work, she suddenly realized she'd forgotten to pick up her child from daycare, and left in a panic. When our attention isn't focused, we can miss a lot, and anything can happen during that time. Look away for a couple seconds while driving on a highway and we've missed the distance of a football field. We often misjudge our control over situations and events, and have a sort of delusion that we are logical all the time.

This should scare business leaders. When we believe that our perception is reality, we're deceiving ourselves. Under this mirage, we might take actions that result in significant mistakes. It doesn't matter what our credentials are or how many years of experience we have. Logic can fail. And when it does, bad things happen.

MENTAL ERRORS

In the documentary *The Fog of War,* Robert S. McNamara states "belief and seeing are both often wrong." McNamara was the U.S. Secretary of Defence under Presidents Kennedy and Johnson. He was actively involved in the Cuban Missile Crisis and then the Vietnam War, which came to be dubbed "McNamara's War" and resulted in the deaths of 3.4 million Vietnamese people and 58,220 U.S. soldiers.

During the Cuban Missile Crisis, the United States had a very good understanding of the enemy; one of President Kennedy's advisors had been an ambassador to Russia and knew Nikita Khrushchev well. But the U.S. did not understand Vietnam nearly as deeply. It was the Cold War, and the U.S. perceived the West as under the threat of Communism and was determined to stop its spread. In the documentary, McNamara recalls a conversation he had with the foreign minister of Vietnam. The minister expressed to McNamara that Vietnam was not a pawn of Russia or China; all they wanted was their independence. They believed the U.S. wanted to exert colonial power over them, just as the French had, so they were willing to fight to maintain that independence. So, in fact, the West was under no threat at all from Vietnam. The U.S. government's premise for going to war was wrong. It was one of many wrong assumptions throughout the course of this war.

With an incomplete understanding of reality, assumptions fill in the blanks. Not seeing the whole story, and seeing only what we want to believe, leads to biases. Finding bits of information to confirm our beliefs, and being under the influence of "group think"—the social dynamics of going along with others that discourages individual responsibility—creates the circumstances for wrong conclusions. And in the case of the Vietnam War, a lot of people lost their lives because of that kind of thinking. At the end of the documentary, McNamara describes what the fog of war is. "War is so complex and beyond the human mind to understand all of the variables. Our judgment and understanding aren't adequate and we will kill people unnecessarily." He continues: "It isn't [that] we aren't rational ... reason has limits."

Today, things haven't changed. Because *we* haven't changed. Wrong decisions are still made based on misconceptions, biases, and assumptions. Beliefs are reinforced in the mind through our actions. We can get caught up in our beliefs and miss signals and feedback from our external environment. Too often, only when bad outcomes hit do aspects of reality come to our attention. But at that point, it's too late to go back. So, we need to get better at bringing awareness to what we *think* we see and believe. We must question what is actually happening right now. Even then, we may only ever see a fraction of reality.

When Deepwater Horizon, an oil drilling rig operated by the BP oil and gas company in the Gulf of Mexico, exploded in April 2010, 11 people died. It was the largest oil spill during marine drilling; four million barrels of oil poured out for 87 days. The extent of the devastation after more than a decade remains unknown, but damage was so broad it covered the entire northern Gulf of Mexico. Ultimately it was determined that the blast was caused by the failure of a seal on the blowout preventer system, which is the last defence against an explosion. It's designed to stop the expanding gaseous hydrocarbons filling up a well. But that wasn't the only mistake:

engineers and other workers made a series of mistakes leading up to the explosion.

BP had smashed records for the deepest well ever constructed. The Deepwater Horizon drilling operation was a highly complex, risky job with many partners, workers, and stakeholders, yet the rig had a seven-year track record without any serious accidents. BP was leasing the rig from Switzerland-based Transocean Ltd., who had provided a highly reputable expert crew. It sounds like a recipe for success, yet disaster struck. Despite all of their years of experience, expertise, and technology, the crew didn't spot the signs of a looming catastrophe. Why didn't they see the explosion coming? How could they have missed these critical signs?

Sidney Dekker, a Dutch psychologist who studies large technological breakdowns, says BP's mishap was a series of repeated small mistakes and misjudgments that, when not caught, escalated into something bigger and far worse. BP had made decisions that prioritized speed, so they cut corners. Past successes resulted in their overconfidence, causing them to gloss over things and get sucked into a false sense of reality. When the red flags appeared, they were normalized with assumptions.

All of this led to the final and fatal oversight: the problem with the blowout preventer. BP did two pressure tests to determine whether the well was sealed or not. The first test was concerning, so they did a second test on a different pipe, and it looked fine. They paid more attention to that second test, and based on that, assumed all was under control. Ignoring the data that didn't fit their expectations left them in shambles because they couldn't react fast enough to stop the accident after oil and mud poured out onto the rig floor. At that point, the explosion was inevitable.

Expert sociologist Diane Vaughan has a theory called normalization of deviance. She describes it in her book *The Challenger Launch Decision*, in which she delved into the 1986 *Challenger* space shuttle accident that killed seven people. Normalization of deviance, she says, describes high-risk industries as being prone to normalizing pushing boundaries. She writes that NASA officials systematically deluded themselves by redefining, early in the shuttle program, what constituted a safe leak in the booster rockets' rubber seals, concluding that small leaks were fine as long as they didn't go beyond a particular threshold. "They redefined evidence that deviated from an acceptable standard so that it *became* the standard," Vaughan writes. As shuttle missions continued, the leaks increased in size, and so what was considered safe also increased. There was a false sense of security. On the day *Challenger* launched, cold temperatures made the rubber brittle, and there was a catastrophic leak.

We see normalization of deviance in business all the time. Managers focus on good data while putting aside or not paying attention to bad data. And so, small decisions are made that inch away from policy and rules. These acceptances increase risk, leaving signs of trouble lurking in the abyss. Beliefs start to seep into the culture that all is okay, and people make assumptions based on that. It all *looks* normal, so nothing is wrong.

In the Deepwater Horizon disaster, BP and Transocean assumed nothing would go wrong, while at the same time making decisions that increased risks. Researchers say that after long periods of no accidents, people form expectations in their mind of safe operations. The assumptions show up as a norm, and experienced employees and leaders will succumb to making errors by not recognizing risks.

BP pled guilty to felony counts related to the deaths of 11 workers, and settled civil and criminal penalties of $20.8 billion. But the Deepwater Horizon catastrophe left a far wider path of destruction. The long-term health impact for those who aided in the cleanup and who live on or near the Gulf Coast remains unclear, but one Louisiana physician described it as "the biggest public health crisis from a chemical poisoning in the history of this country." As for the environmental impact: One scientist estimates that the habitats on the Gulf's floor could take decades or hundreds of years to fully recover. And the economic impacts were also devastating to Gulf Coast sectors such as offshore drilling, fishing, and tourism. Lost tourism dollars alone were estimated at more than $22 billion in 2013.

Our thoughts set the course for what we want to see and believe. But the fact that these ideas could be wrong, and conceived from faulty thinking, fools leaders into believing they're doing the right thing when instead they have done the wrong thing. They've created a false reality based on biases and assumptions.

BEWARE OF HEURISTICS

We know the mind is not as rational as we believe. It is prone to error, and that will never change. Once, while working in a financial institution, I took over a business case (approved by the executive team) to replace technology at a bargain price tag of $800,000. After reviewing the business case, my instinct pulled my attention to some red flags. I told a director on my team that we needed to reassess everything, and even though we were on a tight deadline, I felt that taking the time to closely review the business case was the right thing to do. Our review surfaced assumptions that didn't add up and key items that were missing. So we interviewed stakeholders, reviewed old documents, and spoke to technology partners to develop a revised business case. The new price tag was $7.8 million—almost ten times the original cost. I explained it all to the executive team, sharing clear assumptions and critical facets of reality that weren't represented before. They were astonished, but they understood, and we got the green light to go ahead.

When we have a lot on the go, pressure can build to get things done. We take shortcuts, miss details, and create assumptions to force reality into making sense. So we need to learn how to bring awareness to our thinking and the way we perceive things, rather than assume that what we see are facts and represent the entirety of something. Rushing to complete a task creates mounting pressure on the brain, which is inundated with information; it is constantly trying to simplify things and help get us through the day by using tried and true rules of thumb.

These mental shortcuts have a name: heuristics. Psychologists say heuristics play a significant role in how we understand and respond to experiences. I know it sounds like jargon, but it's important to understand this concept because, while mental shortcuts reduce the complexity of what's taking place and help us to assess probabilities and values much more easily, quick decisions aren't always the right decisions. Let's say you're in your car and in a hurry to get somewhere. You find yourself at an intersection waiting to make a left turn. You need to decide if you have enough time to turn before the car coming the other way reaches the intersection. The fact you are in a hurry means you could rush to make that judgment—leaving yourself vulnerable to error.

There are three types of heuristics you need to know about: representativeness, availability, and adjustment and anchoring.

Representative Heuristic: "It worked before, so it must work again."

I've done the Grouse Grind in Vancouver, which is about a 3-kilometre hike going straight up Grouse Mountain, with an elevation of 850 metres. When I was visiting Abbotsford, my sister asked if I wanted to do the Abby Grind at Sumas Mountain. I knew that mountain was smaller and a shorter distance so I said yes (after all, my expectations had been formed by my experience doing the Grouse Grind). This is the representativeness heuristic, which assesses the likelihood of an outcome. We compare how similar an event is to something else. For instance, imagine you have to decide on allocating a project budget. You review proposals for allocating the dollars to new technology, or hiring talent, or improving business processes. Thoughts come into your mind about what led to good results during a past experience. It worked before, so it must work again, and you make your decision.

That might be a problem. We tend to overvalue the similarities between situations. In a project proposal scenario, we may assume the path to a past success will be the best one for the current project. That causes us to ignore other relevant information. Sometimes, we get put in a tough position in the absence of information. So, we rely on our experience. We categorize information to help make sense of the world around us, and that leads us to see similarities. I assumed the Abby Grind would be like the Grouse Grind, with some stairs and a solid trail underfoot. Well, the trail had no stairs and was so dry and dusty that on the way back down the mountain, my sisters and I, along with their kids, all slipped and fell at least once. My poor youngest nephew tumbled many times and slid almost the whole way down. Indeed, the trails have some clear differences. We escaped injury, but not the dirt that covered us from head to toe.

Availability Heuristic: "The thing that is most top-of-mind is what matters."

The availability heuristic estimates the probability of an event based on the first piece of information that pops into our mind. So, whatever thoughts emerge most easily must be true. We assume something happens a lot if we can quickly come up with ideas or think of many examples. But that makes us overestimate things and miss pertinent pieces of information. People are afraid of dying in a shark attack, but the probability of being fatally struck by lightning is far greater. Movies have vilified sharks as predators that attack humans so we can easily imagine it. Certain risks can get overestimated while others get underestimated. Insurance is an example: People who have just experienced a natural disaster may immediately buy more insurance coverage, but years later they will reduce their coverage—even though the disaster risk is the same.

When critical risks aren't top of mind, we can overlook them. Just look at COVID-19. In 2018, how many organizations had a global pandemic on their risk register? That example can be applied broadly. Once, while working on a technology project, I was collaborating with the organization's risk team. The risk events we identified were a total system failure and a natural disaster at the location of the technology provider in Ohio. My colleagues and teams said at the time that these were "black swan" events that would never happen. But they did happen—both of them. The company's systems went down for three excruciating days, and the technology partner experienced a hurricane that forced relocation to a disaster recovery site.

Just as politicians can get people to believe something if they repeat it enough, business leaders can fall into the trap of believing something to be true because they keep hearing it. For example, leaders can get caught in this mental error when managing talent. Let's say we hear high praise about a particular employee and, because of that, we also praise them. Meanwhile, other good performers go unnoticed because we don't hear about them. Giving weight to what first comes to mind also influences our thoughts about the future. The availability heuristic can make us believe what's going on now will continue.

Adjustment and Anchoring Heuristic: "The starting point is the right starting point."

My car was in for a routine service. I got a call from a service representative who said the car needed some repairs. Part of its suspension was broken and a belt was about to snap. He quoted a cost of $2,600.

Naturally, I was annoyed. I thought I was getting a routine oil change. He then told me he'd give me a discount and the new cost would be $2,000. Because the initial price was in my head, the new one sounded reasonable.

This illustrates the adjustment and anchoring heuristic at work. It estimates value based on a starting point. That value may get adjusted up or down, but the initial value remains the anchor that influences the decision-making process. The problem is that it can very well be an insufficient starting point. Relying on the first piece of information skews how we think through the decision. Negotiations often have this heuristic at play. The same goes for when we meet someone new. If that first impression was positive, that's how we will consider the relationship. But if it was a negative experience, we will continue to have a dim view of the individual.

Circumstances that cause us to rush decision-making influence the bias. Being cramped for time is one cause. For example, if we run out of time in a meeting and cut the discussion short, we and our colleagues might skip identifying and evaluating options. The other cause is a lack of motivation; we won't put in the cognitive effort if we are disengaged or feel lazy. But while whizzing through decisions in order to just move on makes leaders feel good and productive, it's not actually productive. Leaders like having the answers and responding even though they might not know. Lacking knowledge and reverting to guesswork mean we'll fall victim to this heuristic. Without cognitive effort, we don't engage in critical thought that could lead to better decisions.

HOW TO AVOID MENTAL ERRORS

- *Become aware that you are using heuristics.* Research says that when people become aware they are using a heuristic they often change their initial judgment.

- *Be open to experiences.* This will make you less prone to mental errors because you will consider new information. Avoid a closed attitude and remaining fixed in your thoughts.

- *Understand your emotional state.* If your mood is low, you can be susceptible to heuristics. Your brain is already bogged down by your emotional state, so you will have fewer cognitive resources available for critical thinking.

- *Remember that collective thinking is more powerful than individual thinking.* Debate ideas with colleagues and employees, and invite different perspectives. You will encourage your mind to consider more than just the first piece of information.

- *Avoid quick decisions*, and use decision-making tools that guide you to consider alternatives and integrate different viewpoints to arrive at conclusions. Avoid using anchors in decision-making if it's not beneficial.

- *Clear your mind of any mental clutter when making decisions.* If your mind is full with many scattered thoughts, your thinking will not be focused.

- *If you don't have the information or knowledge, say so.* Find people and sources that can support the decision-making processes. Being transparent encourages others

> to demonstrate the same behaviour. You can better piece together the information that you collectively know and don't know, and find ways to close the gaps.

COGNITIVE BIASES

Even more dangerous than heuristics is the fact that we have around 180 cognitive biases that can emerge at any point. Three of the most common cognitive, or conscious, biases include confirmation bias, actor–observer bias, and sunk-cost fallacy.

Confirmation bias is searching for and focusing on information that supports our beliefs; we ignore facts and discount information that does not conform to our ideas. The bias makes us believe we are right. Leaders are highly susceptible to this bias, especially the higher they go up the corporate ladder, where they might not get feedback telling them they're lacking perspective and not considering pertinent data.

Actor–observer bias leads us to assume that our actions result from external factors beyond our control; for example, if we miss a deadline, we attribute that to having too much work. Yet when peers miss deadlines, we might assume the cause is internal, that perhaps our colleague has poor time-management skills. Employee performance reviews and leadership meetings to decide an employee's final rating grossly influences this bias. I have witnessed (and I'm sure you have, too) situations when the performance of one employee is justified and that of another person in the exact same circumstances is not. This kind of bias can unfairly affect someone's career and pay.

Sunk-cost fallacy encourages us to push forward with actions even if they might create adverse outcomes. Leaders slip into this bias with ease. I took over some work on a team that was developing a small-business credit product. The team had been working on it for about a year and a half. I sat down with the employees leading the work and felt that their solution didn't make any sense. The back end was so clunky that there was a high potential it would create a horrible customer experience. Plus, there were administrative errors. I decided to cancel the project because, despite all the time invested and costs incurred, it was the right decision. Turning away from time, money, and resources already spent is hard. It feels like a waste, even if the outcome would not be good. When we get attached to resources spent, it's tough to gain the perspective that, in the end, we won't succeed.

UNCONSCIOUS BIASES

Unconscious biases happen when the brain triggers processes to make quick judgments and assessments about people and situations. The brain does this automatically, and we can't control it. Thus, it allows the brain to perceive, filter information, and make decisions essential for survival—all based on our personal background, experiences, memories, and cultural environment. The brain forms predictive models and uses associations, patterns, and generalities to tag and store information. This kind of use of our experiences and knowledge in the moment helps us make split-second decisions and function without overload.

We can't change the innate nature of the brain to function with unconscious bias. Yet, we do need to understand how it affects the way we see the world and influences our responses. Take first impressions, for example. When we meet new people, the brain's unconscious processes get underway, with different regions in the brain becoming active in familiar and unfamiliar situations. Let's say an intern is joining your company for the summer. After you encounter them, the prefrontal cortex region of the brain gets active. It monitors information and references social norms and preferences. At this point, stereotypes and labels get applied. Perhaps thoughts cross your mind that the person is young and therefore must lack experience. You then think you will have to spend more time training them than getting work output. Your brain makes these decisions in the subconscious. Then, it enters conscious awareness, where the thinking is slower and more controlled. Your brain has associated a young person with not having enough experience—even though you don't know what expertise, training, or background they have actually brought.

The amygdala region of the brain labels and categorizes information. It considers "like me," "unlike me," and "in-group" or "out-group." When we meet someone new, these processes check if the person is like us. We are biased toward people similar to us, and we like them more than others. The amygdala also plays a critical role in assessing threat levels. It enables us to make quick decisions and act. If we're walking in a dark alleyway and hear a noise, we decide to walk faster. That's the amygdala in action. But remember, this brain region categorizes and filters information. Thus, it results in biases and prejudices that associate with threat and fear. These unconscious processes work as they should. Whatever happens around us seeps into our minds without our awareness. We remain susceptible to biases. Yet, we can change them through new experiences and learning.

> **HOW TO BE AWARE OF BIAS—AND AVOID IT**
>
> - *Uncover and acknowledge your biases.* You can take a test by Project Implicit (a collaboration among universities) that measures your attitudes and beliefs. This will help give you a sense of your biases—awareness is a critical step.
> - *Be open to learning and discovering new information to shift how you think.* When we experience new things, it can change the structure of the brain. New social attitudes and changed expectations can alter how the brain processes information. Your brain will begin to retrieve a different set of memories to form conclusions.
> - *Bring transparency if you spot biases in your organization.* Consider it an ongoing learning journey to understand the circumstances and scenarios where biases appear. For instance, be mindful of first impressions and question extreme views about employees. Biases are learned through environments, so everyone has a responsibility to counteract them.
> - *Meet and work with people who are different from you.* You will learn more about others that could change how you think about generalizations and stereotypes. Encourage employees to share their perspectives.

- *Slow down decision-making* and pay attention to processes for hiring, recruitment, promotions, job assignments, customer service, and investment decisions.

MENTAL MODELS

We make sense of and interact with the world through mental models. These are internal representations of external reality, and they come from our experiences, perceptions, and understanding of the world. Think of them as deep-rooted assumptions that form the basis of reasoning. For example, supply and demand is a dominant mental model that business leaders apply to understand and set competitive prices. It helps them grasp complexity of markets. The law of diminishing returns is another mental model that helps us understand when our efforts will eventually produce fewer results; in turn, that helps us make decisions without analyzing reams of information.

Mental models support our interaction with reality by providing a simplified view. That helps with reasoning, anticipating events, and forming explanations of what we witness. The models also act as a filter for new information. So we develop and use mental models to help us understand and function daily. Yet we tend to lack awareness of the mental models we use. We don't recognize how these constructs affect our thoughts and behaviours and how we perceive moment-to-moment reality.

No wonder leaders disregard risks: when mental models block out things that don't fit, we understand only parts of what's happening, get misled by confidence—and make wrong, costly decisions. Because when the landscape changes, we miss critical information or lose out on insights that create new ways to think.

Pan American Airways took to the skies at the start of the Great Depression but was relegated to the history books six decades later. The decline of what was then the world's largest international air carrier is a clear example of leadership that couldn't see that its own view of reality was faulty. It wasn't always that way. Pan Am was an industry pioneer: the first to fly internationally, the first to adopt jumbo jets, and the first to use computerized reservation systems. But for some reason, in 1980—after a decade that saw an oil embargo, a slowing economy, and lower demand for air travel that left the company with mounting debt—Pan Am decided to set its sights on domestic expansion and purchased National Airlines for $437 million. It overpaid, and the acquisition didn't go well, so Pan Am had no choice but to sell assets. The company tried again to expand into the domestic market, but after a deal to merge with Northwest Airlines failed, it had no choice but to file for bankruptcy in 1991.

Why didn't leadership stay focused on the company's strengths as an international carrier? With its cashflow problems, why didn't Pan Am hold off and wait for the right time for expansion? It makes you wonder what world it saw that led them down this path; clearly, it was a faulty view of reality. Pan Am didn't evolve its mental models to reflect what was evolving both in the external environment and the internal one (with issues such as acquisition failures and an accumulation of debt). Perhaps leadership was misled with confidence, thinking that a company with such a long history of success was invincible even in a much-changed economy. The moral of this story: Leaders need to bring attention to mental models that drive their beliefs about strategic choices and what changes in the external environment mean. We need to question our views that have formed long-held assumptions that could be out of context with reality.

Assumptions are one of the biggest causes of mental errors. They're hard to spot, but they can limit your perspectives and quality of thinking without you even knowing it. Failing to identify assumptions takes away the chance to understand what's looming. Take Target. The U.S.-based retailer assumed it could apply the same formula of its success to Canada. But it was wrong: Just one year after ambitiously entering the Canadian market in 2023, Target Canada had lost US$941 million. Bankrupt by January 2015, it had to close 133 stores, and 17,600 people lost their jobs.

Many challenges doomed Target Canada. Reports revealed problems with technology, products, supply chains, and distribution, and many of the problems were caused by wrong assumptions. For one, Target assumed its brand alone was enough to win Canadian customers; after all, it had long been a popular cross-border shopping destination. But Canadians found that the products on the shelves weren't the same as the products in the U.S., and the customer service wasn't as good either. Products were not reaching stores—errors in managing the inventory and supply chain caused the delays—while the distribution centres remained overstocked. Systems that forecast and replenish inventory use years of historical data to estimate sales, but Target Canada didn't have this information, so it used assumptions from its U.S. operations.

The mistakes piled up. The company had assumed Canada was similar to the United States, so it didn't account for simple differences such as currency or the fact that Canada uses the metric system, which meant there would be differences in store shelving sizes.

Opaque assumptions leave us unprepared for what might go wrong. We don't grasp what's taking place around us. Proceeding with actions without awareness reinforces our mental models. The status quo continues when we get caught up in busy days and don't have time to think. As a result, bias forms in how we view our business and the steps we take. Our organization falls into trouble, and yet we can't do anything about it if we're attached to the past and our way of seeing things. So we won't listen to new ideas. We don't notice the trends and how to evolve with changing needs.

In the late 1800s, Kodak began innovating with the world's first fully portable camera. Capturing most of the market share in the United States, Kodak enjoyed decades of success. In January 2012, Kodak filed for bankruptcy protection. One major reason was the introduction of the digital camera to the mass market in 1990. The digital camera represented a massive shift requiring a new business model. But the company ignored this. (Ironically, in 1975, one of Kodak's own engineers invented the digital camera. It was the size of a toaster. Someone told the engineer, "That's cute, but don't tell anyone about it.") When Kodak acquired the photo-sharing website Ofoto in 2001, the opportunity to pivot from traditional photography was right in front of them. But it dismissed the idea of thinking about consumer needs in a different way. Instead, Kodak remained deeply tied to the belief that consumers wanted to print digital images. The arrival of the smartphone proved that assumption was wrong. Kodak's success in photography cemented its desire to preserve the same business. It failed to see how digital innovations would overhaul the industry and consumer behaviour; deeply rooted beliefs about its consumers and photography shaped that perception. And so, Kodak created resistance and paralyzed its own ability to see how the world would evolve.

We need mental models to function. But bringing our awareness to them is paramount. Pan Am didn't evolve its mental models to face what was happening internally and externally. Target Canada made several bad assumptions. And Kodak stayed attached to an old idea and remained stuck in its beliefs. We must appreciate the forces that influence perceptions and shape our thoughts and actions. If we understand only parts of the reality taking place, we can't do our best thinking. We remain limited in thoughts, behaviours, and actions. If we appreciate the subjective nature of reality, we'll be better able to comprehend what's behind our thoughts, and the result will be truly effective decisions. Mental models reflect our goals and motives. We *can* change them. But first, we need to understand our conscious experience and how perception works.

> **HOW TO SEE YOUR OWN MENTAL MODELS**
>
> There are countless mental models, and we use them in everyday reasoning. They allow us to infer and predict events. Getting familiar with your mental models will really help you to become aware of how you think. Don't worry about trying to determine all of your mental models—that is impossible. However, you

can create practices for yourself to get deeper insight about the beliefs and assumptions that influence how you think, behave, and act. The following are a few key steps you can take.

- *Question yourself and challenge your thinking.* You can also challenge the thinking of others since we are also influenced by others.
- *Bring your attention to assumptions.* How did you arrive at a conclusion? Consider it like showing your work when you solve a math problem. The final answer is not the only aspect that's important; it's also how you got there.
- *Try to suspend assumptions* and avoid the temptation to jump to conclusions.
- *Understand your thought patterns to uncover habitual thinking and deeply held beliefs.* You can unlearn those things and learn new ways to think.
- *Remember that mental models are not static.* They constantly evolve based on experiences. Get out of your comfort zone and make it a regular practice to keep learning new things.
- *Become aware of how you interpret the world and the way it affects your life.* This will help you see your beliefs and their influence on how you function.

HOW TO SURFACE ASSUMPTIONS IN A MEETING

Deep-rooted assumptions can be like weeds that don't stop growing. One belief leads us to the next, to the point where the rationale of actions is unclear. A problem unfolds and we have no idea how we got into a sticky mess. When leaders lack awareness of the assumptions that are infused in thinking and decisions, we create false confidence that leads to blind spots.

Meetings are a prime conduit for assumptions to go undetected. Establishing a practice to identify and share assumptions with transparency leads to higher-quality thinking, decisions, and actions. Here are some best practices.

- Set the expectation with colleagues to come to meetings prepared to share assumptions they've made.
- At the start of agenda topics, ask attendees to share their assumptions. Those who struggled to identify theirs will benefit from the experience; it's easier to build on the ideas of others.
- As you go through the meeting and arrive at conclusions, ask the group if any of the assumptions have changed. Make note of what comes up.
- Following the meeting, it's good practice to document and share assumptions with teams. Assumptions greatly impact how employees work given that they can change and evolve their mental models.

The mind can experience many pitfalls throughout the day. Consequences will vary from minor things going wrong to severe damage. If we miss parts of reality, we can make mistakes. If we make quick judgments, we can make mistakes. If we don't have awareness of our beliefs, we can make mistakes. With all these potential mental errors, we must avoid self-doubting. Instead, we must become conscious of our mental errors by recruiting different parts of ourselves to help.

I THINK, THEREFORE I AM?

For millennia, human beings have tried to understand consciousness. In Ancient Greece, philosophers Plato and Aristotle studied human consciousness. They explored the depths of human nature and the soul. Aristotle was Plato's student. He created some of the most influential works on consciousness and perception. In those days, people believed the heart was the seat of sensation, will, and the soul.

Later, in the 17th century, French philosopher and father of modern philosophy René Descartes created a new perspective: "I think, therefore I am." His work led to the modern view of consciousness. The focus shifted from the heart to the relationship between mind and body. For centuries, this perspective has dominated. Now, years of scientific research and theories on consciousness have led to greater insights about the brain. We know more about how we perceive reality: that the perception of reality is subjective and depends on the individual person, and how the consciousness of human beings compares to other living things.

Research and debate continue. This tells me that consciousness flows in the brain but also arises in the body through feelings. So, here's my definition:

Consciousness comes from the brain, body, feelings, and intuition interacting in the moment-to-moment experience. Awareness of the subjective experience is continuously influenced by our conscious and unconscious interpretation of it.

Consciousness starts with our perception of reality. We need to consider how much we really notice in the moment-to-moment experience. Every human being has their version of what they believe is reality. With a global population of eight billion, there are eight billion realities happening right now. What is the version of truth? Well, there isn't only one. Whatever we notice in the moment guides what we see, think, feel, and do. That's different from our colleagues, partner, and family. Our attention has a significant influence over what we experience. Where we place our attention is what we notice and perceive. The brain takes directive and follows with unconscious and conscious processes to make sense of the moment.

Mark Solms, author of *The Hidden Spring*, says overwhelming evidence indicates that we are mostly unaware of what we perceive and learn. When moments unfold, we perceive what's happening by the brain's predictions. The brain predicts based on information stored in long-term memory. It's as if we are seeing a movie of the world around us, rather than the actual world. And that movie is directed by our memory of the events of our past. In that sense, the past is always with us in the present. The influence on beliefs and how we behave in the moment happens without notice.

In *Thinking, Fast and Slow*, Daniel Kahneman, a Nobel prize–winning psychologist, explains the unconscious and conscious parts of the mind as System 1 and System 2. System 1 is fast. It operates quickly and on automatic, requiring little or no effort from us. We're not aware of it. System 2 is slow. It is the slower conscious mind. We use this part to identify who we are. System 2 holds our beliefs and helps us reason and make choices. The slower conscious mind also helps to allocate our attention to mental activities. These types of tasks require effort, such as complex problem-solving. The two systems work in harmony to make the moment-to-moment experiences flow together.

System 1 quietly makes continuous suggestions for System 2. The unconscious mind shares feelings, impressions, intentions, and intuitions. System 2 usually adopts the recommendations of System 1 with few or no changes. The conscious mind's endorsement turns impressions and intuitions into beliefs. It also turns impulses into voluntary actions. So much for our assumption that we are rational beings. When System 1 runs into a challenge it can't solve, it calls on System 2. The conscious mind steps in to help with processing and solving the problem. We're aware of it when System 2, the slow one, steps in, but most of the time System 1, the fast one, is in the driver's seat.

Our reaction to how we perceive reality starts outside of conscious awareness. There's nothing concrete about reality, yet we treat it that way. So we must learn to shift our awareness to how we interpret reality and expand our understanding of it.

GET OUT OF YOUR HEAD

How we experience reality depends on the way we engage in the moment. It comes back to our conscious awareness of the experience. If we are in our head, we'll see part of reality, but we'll miss out on a lot. That can lead to mistakes and bad decisions. So what can we do?

What if we listened to our feelings? Say, that nagging awareness that something is amiss. Call it gut instinct. If we pay attention to our feelings, they can act like a great coach. They can give insight into our behaviour and prompt self-inquiry. We're bound to discover something relevant that makes our thinking better.

In the chapters that follow, we will explore the ways we can expand our awareness, to see more but still listen to our feelings—our heart and our gut. That will free us from the trap of our mind. We will make better decisions without habitual thought patterns blocking new thoughts. Also, we will become better leaders, taking stronger actions based on our understanding of experiences. The subjective experience will always remain that way, but by tuning into our self and knowing there is subjectivity, we can change our perspectives. Our awareness helps us shift what we perceive. And that could change our world.

KEY TAKEAWAYS

- *The mind is prone to mistakes and is not as rational as we tend to think.* Distractions and multitasking can cause mistakes. The brain can fail to process information.

- *Rules of thumb that we create simplify reality and make it easier to get through the day.* But they can be the source of error. There are three main types: 1) We compare how similar the event is to something else and overestimate the likelihood of it happening again. 2) We assess the probability or risk based on what comes to mind. 3) We estimate value based on some arbitrary starting point to come to a final answer.

- *Mental models help us to make sense of and interact with the world.* They're based on deep-rooted assumptions and help us to reason, anticipate events, explain experiences, and assess new information. They can cause us to reject information if it doesn't fit.

- *Mental models lead to habitual thought patterns, which reinforce how we see the world.* They limit how we pay attention, and cause us to miss critical information or lose out on observations and new insights. The result is that we can only understand pieces of what's happening. We can get misled by our confidence and make ineffective decisions due to a lack of awareness.

- *Assumptions live in mental models.* Failing to identify assumptions takes away the chance to understand what's beneath. We won't know what's influencing our thinking.

- *Perception shapes how we experience reality.* Every person has their version of what they believe is happening. What we notice in the moment directs what we see, think, feel, and do.
- *Consciousness flows in the brain and arises in the body through feelings.* It comes from the brain, body, feelings, and intuition interacting in the moment-to-moment experience. Awareness of the subjective experience is continuously influenced by our conscious and unconscious interpretation of it.

Step 1: Be Present

In 2017, I was completing my Executive MBA. Our class was filled with working professionals juggling full-time jobs, school, and life priorities. One day right after the new year, we dove into corporate finance—and that was the day the professor's patience with us broke. He was teaching us the weighted average cost of capital (WACC) formula and writing it out on the whiteboard. When he turned around to face us, he lost it. He told one of my colleagues to stop talking because they were annoying everyone. He told another to stop playing with his new Christmas toy, an Apple watch. Another was working on a real-estate deal, as he often did. I realized that each of us was distracted in some way. Then the professor said something that I never forgot. He told us that we were deteriorating our attentional capacity, and because of that, we weren't learning. That day, we were told to put our devices away and our pens down to learn WACC.

With so much happening around us all the time, it's hard to be present. Everywhere we go, we are overloaded with stimuli. No matter how many goals we set ourselves to be productive, they mean nothing if we are always distracted and unfocused.

Much can go amiss when we don't pay attention in every moment. I'm an avid hiker, and the things that must stay top of mind for me are to regularly look ahead at the trail so that I know what's coming and so I don't take a wrong turn. But it's just as crucial that I also keep my eyes on the ground so I don't trip on loose rocks or tree roots. Golfers, too, know the importance of focus: You can't rush the shot. Your attention needs to be laser-focused on the complete process of the swing, from head to toe. You can't worry about the next hole, and you can't think about your score. And cyclists are all too aware that only if you're in the moment at all times can you prevent wipeouts. You have to be fully aware of your surroundings, the route, the road surface. Focus makes us successful at whatever we're doing.

Lindsey Vonn, a retired alpine skier with three Olympic gold medals and World Cup wins, set herself up for success with an unwavering focus. She has said that when you're going 80 miles an hour, you have to be 100 percent focused on what you're doing. You can't think about anything else. Vonn was able to do that, and to see exactly where she needed to go. There was no space to think about anything else. On the mountain, she was present and so she succeeded.

But it's tough to stay present. One minute you're working on a task. The next, your mind drifts away, and even though you have told yourself to focus, it doesn't help. Like me, you have probably been in meetings where you tune in and out of the conversation. You scribble down some notes, respond to emails, and chime in a few times. You remind yourself to pick up a few items from the grocery store after work. The upcoming weekend pops into your mind. These thoughts come to an abrupt stop when a comment catches your attention. You glance around the room, then nod in agreement to *what you think you heard*.

We all experience these moments, and the result. When reading an email, we miss a critical sentence. While conversing with a colleague, we neglect to hear about a task our team needs to finish. Reading a financial report, we miss a zero. This has become normalized.

We often hear that the top leadership skills include being a visionary, a strategic thinker, and a good communicator. Resilience and adaptability are known leadership qualities, too, and charisma is on the list. More recently, showing vulnerability has become a profound way to improve leadership. But none of those things matter if we don't know how to direct our attention. That means that attention is the most important leadership skill.

We need our full ability to focus to the world around us, yet that's challenging to sustain. Even if we *think* we're present as we go about our day, we can easily miss what's taking place. So, why is it so hard to focus?

THE MYTH OF MULTITASKING

In our modern world, it's hard to pay attention to what counts. We live in a world full of distractions that compete for our attention. Everything from inside the home to when we step outside can split our limited attention into pieces. Add to that emails, text messages, news headlines, and social media—the daily demands pile up fast and, in turn, tempt us to multitask.

Contrary to what many people believe, multitasking doesn't make us more productive. In fact, there's no such thing as multitasking. It's actually task-switching. We learn to do one task and then another. The brain gets very good at switching, making it feel like a seamless and automatic experience. But science proves that we cannot do several tasks very well at the same time. In fact, the brain can't do more than two complex things at once. If we try to introduce a third task, the prefrontal cortex will drop one. So when we try to multitask, all we're doing is disrupting the flow of thoughts and dividing our attention. That makes us slower to respond and vulnerable to mistakes: the brain gets confused, we slow down, and we make errors. On top of that, the brain's amygdala triggers the stress response, which causes our logical reasoning to suffer.

Our attention span has limits, and knowing that is critical. For instance, simply having a conversation uses up half of the brain's attention capacity, according to research. So if we are talking to a client on the phone while working on our computer at the same time, our brain chooses which information to process. In that scenario, because the brain tends to focus most on the thing we're seeing, we'll be more engaged with our computer screen and hear less of what our client is saying. There's a cost to doing more than one thing at a time.

Work environments erode our ability to concentrate on a task. Each workday with packed agendas leaves little room to take a break or just pause for a moment. The pressure to keep up influences a perpetual state of juggling many priorities. What's more, workplace technologies intended to support collaboration actually split team members' attention to their tasks, resulting in errors. For example, task-management programs like Agile encourage teams to multitask. While that might sound like a good idea, loading employees up with various pieces of work only increases the likelihood of errors. Instant-messaging platforms such as Teams may make everyone reachable at any time, but all of that pinging interrupts everyone's attention. Because we aren't able to listen well, we can lose track of what's going on.

We learned to work remotely because of the pandemic. We can now travel around with our desks and work anywhere. The downside is that encourages us to multitask. In meetings, having multiple screens at our fingertips is the norm. And it's not only us multitasking, but possibly everyone else in that meeting. The costs of this is a loss of human connection. When people speak, they might not even receive eye contact from a single person in the room. That's not an engaging environment to spark deep dialogue or get the best out of people. We need to look at one another and notice body language to help us understand messages and more of what's happening. Shallow conversations with no real insights or clarity can leave people with fuzzy thoughts, making action items equally confusing.

Avoid the Temptation to Multitask

Trying to meet competing needs puts us in a position of having to double up on our actions. Devices are one thing, but any extra thing we try to do can be a problem. I commuted to Vancouver for work for many years. Part of my morning routine was drinking coffee while driving, since that was more efficient than having it at home. I was confident in my ability to do these two tasks at once. But one day, I was stopped at a red light sipping coffee, and when the light turned green, I put my cup in the holder without taking my eyes off the road, as I'd done countless times before. But this time I missed. So I looked down for one second—and rear-ended the car in front of me. The driver had put on her brakes. We pulled over. The woman was very upset, and asked me if I knew how to drive. I felt horrible about my silly mistake. All I could say was "I'm sorry."

Studies show that about 25 percent of car crashes come from distracted driving, and it is preventable. Legislation that goes beyond using electronics makes good sense. Some no-nos include tooth-flossing, reading, curling your hair, or eating soup while driving. (Yes, the RCMP in B.C. had enough after a woman got caught eating a bowl of ramen while driving.) Distracted drivers have a slower reaction time. When we perform a task and then switch to another, we still hold information in the brain about what we just did. That leaves mental clutter behind to impair our cognition. If we've finished eating a sandwich and put it aside, our brain is still thinking about that instead of noticing traffic coming to a stop.

How you use your attention is your choice. If you must multitask, do so with intention—and only for low-risk activities—when you know what you are doing and why, and with the understanding that there will be one activity that is not going to get all of your attention. For instance, multitasking while grocery shopping is low risk; the only risk of reading text messages as you shop is forgetting to grab something from your list. At work, too, there could be instances where you are able to distribute your attention to more than one task without much risk; for example, scanning a report for key points rather than reading it carefully. When I was leading Payments at a financial institution, I would scan the audit deficiency report, and then during my meeting with the operations director on my team, I would look for the red items to discuss. But workplace instances of successful multitasking are rare. You'll be far more successful if you can learn new habits.

THE WANDERING MIND

It's natural for the mind to wander. Even if we try to pay attention, we can lose the present moment to distracting thoughts. Mind-wandering is a typical activity of the brain; in fact, for almost half of our waking hours, we're thinking about something other than what we are actually doing. According to Dr. Fred Luskin of Stanford University, about 60,000 thoughts cross our minds daily. And a whopping 90 percent of them are repetitive.

When the mind is not engaged, it occupies itself with more interesting ideas, and so every day the brain completes tasks on auto-pilot. But in this low-effort mode, thoughts can travel into the past and recall memories; reliving them can bring up negative emotions. Or, thoughts can jump into the future as we consider scenarios that may never happen. These what-if contemplations might trigger fears of something that isn't even real, and that creates feelings of worry, anxiety, and stress. When our mind engages in these unnecessary thoughts, we are at a disadvantage because our thought process becomes more prone to errors. Our perception is reduced, and our mood lowers. In short, we're not in the best state to think or make decisions.

Mind-wandering is associated with a default, idle region of the brain. This "default mode network" (DMN) gets active when we lose focus on a task, and when we self-talk. The typical experience of mind-wandering will sound familiar to you: While completing a task, your mind easily drifts into a chain of unrelated thinking without you even being conscious of it. For example, when you're reading a book and you suddenly realize you don't know what you just read. You then notice your thoughts and acknowledge going off-task.

Though mind-wandering can feel normal, we should try to overcome it. Repetitive thoughts don't encourage new thinking, and we miss what's happening in the moment. When our mind is full of this useless thinking, our mental resources are being wasted. Once these pathways exist in the brain, habits form. Yet, we can break wandering thoughts by *paying attention to what we are doing in the present moment*.

Our engagement in what we do significantly influences our experience. Think about that the next time you give your employees monotonous, boring work. Yes, sometimes repetitive work needs to get done, but we can create an internal environment that's uplifting so that employees are less vulnerable to distractions. A person's engagement level depends on how they feel during experiences. When planning team sessions, consider the flow of activities. One of my best practices is preparing a well-defined agenda with outcomes for each agenda item. Simply sharing that with participants lets them know what to expect in the session. That means there is less room in their minds to drift from the present into thoughts that have nothing to do with what you're all trying to achieve.

> **LIVE IN THE MOMENT**
>
> Living in the moment increases our happiness, and the research on mind-wandering supports this notion. To test this idea, psychologists Matthew A. Killingsworth and Daniel T. Gilbert developed an iPhone app that surveyed people's thoughts and activities. The app asked participants to complete a questionnaire randomly throughout the day. Participants rated their happiness on a scale of 1 to 100. They then had to share what they were doing—for example, washing dishes—and whether they were thinking about something other than that activity. The study revealed that people are happiest when thinking about the activity they are engaged in rather than thinking about, say, their next vacation. The predictor of happiness, in other words, comes from whether we match our thoughts to actions.

THE BROADCASTER INSIDE

The voice in our head likes to narrate the experiences of our entire day. For example, say, while travelling in Paris, we visit the Eiffel Tower. Instead of enjoying the scenery, we start thinking about what we will see tomorrow. Our thoughts hijack the experience of what's happening now. Instead of enjoying the moment, we escape to the future. Without effort, internal comments flow—comments about what we see, think, and feel. It's as if a broadcaster lives in our minds and our life is a show. We don't question the internal dialogue because it feels normal. After all, it's our voice.

The mental chatter is constant, and it comes from how we perceive and make sense of the world. Our beliefs and views come through how the mind narrates. The internal dialogue is about anything and everything. Sometimes when I'm driving in Toronto, where I now live, I notice my mental chatter. I'm thinking about something I have to do and making a mental list. Then an observation comes into my mind; for example, one day a flock of pigeons on the road would not get out of the way where I had to make a right turn. I started to think about how the pigeons in Vancouver don't behave like that. I waited patiently, and then as I was ready to go, several food delivery drivers whizzed by, and I started to think about how congested Toronto streets are. My thoughts then went back to my errands, until I drove over a pothole, which made me think about how much wear and tear happens to cars. All random thoughts, all presented by the voice in my head perceiving experiences.

Now, sometimes this voice is quite helpful, like when we're cooking. Our inner voice tells us what ingredients to use, and the order of steps as we complete each action. But if our mind interrupts our focus, the results may not be so tasty. I was making porridge one morning, and I unconsciously allowed my inner narrator to switch to unrelated thoughts about how much my life had changed over the past few years. My breakfast paid the price. Instead of adding cinnamon I used cayenne pepper. A spicy kick was not what I wanted in the morning.

We can mistake the mental chatter as helpful, and it's true that it might surface a good idea or two. But that voice in our head makes us susceptible to losing focus and getting distracted. Our thinking is not as controlled and poised, so we can get carried away. The challenge for leaders is that the voice can get stuck in our head and we begin to comment and judge what colleagues are saying. We then get attached to our ideas while not hearing others, and we show up as a judgmental leader—which is not good for us or anyone we interact with. Keep in mind, when the narrator keeps chiming in, our cognition is unnecessarily occupied and we will miss out on what's happening.

> **TIPS FOR BEING PRESENT AT WORK**
>
> When talking with colleagues, do not mentally critique what they are saying. Also, don't overtake the conversation to state your opinions and what you think is best. Instead, listen with openness, and observe.
>
> When we show up to experiences this way, our mind frees from mental chatter and we observe more. Our senses, feelings, and intuition are engaged, which increases our understanding. We perceive more from ourselves and the environment we're in.
>
> Share your thoughts with your colleagues and, regardless of whether they're positive or negative, be authentic and transparent.

> When we describe our thinking rather than blurt out a single statement, our perspectives are less likely to be perceived by others as negative. We gain so much more when we fully open ourselves to the experience, and those working with us benefit as well because they discover what we are seeing.

ATTENTION IS PRECIOUS

From our earliest days of life, we crave attention. "Watch me!" is a command heard by parents everywhere. Throughout life we humans need to be looked at, acknowledged, and heard, and that applies to our professional lives, too. In performance appraisals, for example, employees want the full attention of their boss. They want to know how they did and what the boss thinks of them. This precious commodity is just as important to give as it is to receive.

Attention directly influences what we experience moment to moment. When we decide what to look at or do, we guide our perception to select what we notice. Then, our brain follows suit by using resources to understand a subset of the experience. We can't process every detail; if we did, the brain would get too overwhelmed to function. So, in every moment we decide what counts—and we block out things that don't count. Let's say you're focusing on a project and you're closing in on the deadline. Normally you're distracted by the loud construction noise that has been going on outside of your office for months, but when you're so focused on meeting your deadline, you are no longer distracted. Your brain has filtered out that stimulus. Paying attention to the job at hand has helped you to be alert and productive.

Attention determines what we see in the world around us. If we're strolling in a park one morning, we might focus on a tree in the distance or on the park bench. That choice will determine how we experience the park that day. Because we didn't notice the raccoon ambling across the grass, it doesn't exist. Attention tells the brain to prioritize the information that's coming in from sensory perception. We take in the experience, and that leads to our understanding. If something doesn't exist for us, then it can't shape what we perceive.

PAY ATTENTION PURPOSEFULLY

As leaders, some of our most critical decisions are made when determining our organization's strategy. We typically look at the external environment and trends as well as our own data to gauge how the business is doing now and to see its future trajectory. Then, when it's time to make important decisions about how to reach the organization's goals, the information we bring into the process will influence our actions.

Where will you focus *your* attention? Let's say you analyzed your customer data and decided to continue focusing on that customer base. But what about the future? Who will your customers be, and what will they need? Bringing your attention to your future customers would change your perception and awareness about them. You would understand their needs and new potential opportunities. These insights could shift your entire strategic approach and your investment decisions.

We have to routinely pay attention to issues that can impede performance. We tend to understand problems based on what's visible, but when we spot only some symptoms, many others get missed—the dangers lurking under that clichéd tip of the iceberg. We can end up making conclusions based on limited understanding. Employee engagement surveys are a typical example of when real issues get glossed over. Leaders get caught up in the areas that received low scores, but what's behind that low score? To learn more, it may pay to shift our attention to spending time with employees and observing interactions. So, just like what we see when we're strolling in the park, our ability to gain awareness of a situation all depends on where we decide to direct our attention.

A long time ago, I was a consulting business analyst at a financial institution. I was tasked with helping the senior business banking leaders to understand why the process for new commercial loans took so long. These were complex deals that could not simply be put through a system; they involved multiple touchpoints. I like to think of these situations as a puzzle with only some pieces visible, and I must discover the rest. The leaders tasked me with finding the inefficiencies causing the delays.

I talked to staff, met with leaders, and assessed performance and reports. Then I started to put everything together. I discovered that the commercial loans process had many steps and connected to three sub-processes, which the team—analysts, account managers, and supervisors—weren't even aware of. All they knew was that things were getting stuck somewhere, and they were frustrated. I also found confusion and a lack of clarity around decision authorities, when to escalate issues, and who does what. So it wasn't just the process that was the problem, it was also the roles and the operating model. When I presented my findings to the leaders, they sat quietly looking at me. They realized I had discovered the whole iceberg, and that what they thought was a quick fix wasn't.

That's how important the power of attention is: If we use our attention like a flashlight we can uncover issues that aren't clearly visible. We might discover that the best solution is entirely different than what we expected. Leaders should question whether they have directed their attention to the right problem.

Seeing the whole iceberg also means finding things that leaders don't always *want* to know about. There's apprehension about these skeletons and possible consequences. But we can't just close the door and pretend something doesn't exist. Attention resources have limitations, and without us even knowing it, distractions can use up our cognitive resources. Since we can't make more attention, we have to strengthen what we have.

HOW TO IMPROVE ATTENTION

Improving our attention isn't like going to the gym, where eventually we'll be able to lift more weight. But if we can learn to use our attention effectively, we are more likely to avoid mistakes. The more present we are, the greater our ability to use our attention. So, our capacity to take in and understand what's happening around us increases. Think of how your management will improve if you see the gorilla on the basketball court (see page 1).

Making better decisions helps us be better leaders. We can improve our attention by practising the following.

1. **Learn to focus on one critical task at a time.** Start by reducing distractions. Give yourself space to engage in your activity. As you do, align your thoughts with your actions. The more your thoughts sync up with what you're doing, the easier it becomes to build new habits. This allows different expectations to form in the brain. You learn to home in on what you're doing. In an environment full of distractions, your mind gets used to the stops and starts of working. You won't notice that your productivity level isn't that great. Once you start focusing on your task, you will improve the quality of your thinking and what you produce. After all, you're making good use of cognitive resources. You'll be more aware of the stops and starts, and adjust accordingly. You end up reinforcing behaviours that respect your focus instead of splitting it apart.

2. **Reduce mind-wandering and unnecessary mental chatter.** These overflowing thoughts take up space in your brain, crowding it and wasting its limited resources. You can break mind-wandering simply by being aware that it will happen. When it does, notice the mental train of thought that distracts you. Then bring your mind back to the present. With practice, you will get better at this. Whatever activity or situation you participate in, let the experience happen. When you are able to avoid getting caught in the

mind's chatter, you'll find it's quiet, and that you have more capacity for purposeful thinking. Your brain's expectations shift, and you get pulled out of auto-pilot. You can process more of your surroundings. Gathering information becomes its priority instead of quick judgments and assumptions. And having a few extra moments to process what's happening allows you to ponder before you react.

OBSERVE THE MIND

One way to support our attention is by learning to observe the mind. The practices of mindfulness and meditation can help us do this because they encourage being in the moment and paying attention to our actions. This helps us to notice our thoughts, feelings, and sensations, and use all of our senses to observe the world around us and how we affect it. Mindfulness can also help us detect when our attention has slipped so we can bring it back to whatever we are doing.

Mindfulness can be practised at any time. Mindfulness and meditation are proven by science to produce neuroplasticity changes. The physical changes in the brain enable us to sustain attention to the present.

Mindfulness is a core element of meditation. Meditation helps quiet the mind and clear out mental chatter. To meditate, we direct our attention either inward or on an object for a specific amount of time. There are two primary types of meditation practice: open monitoring and focused attention. With open-monitoring meditation, we observe our thoughts and experiences with non-judgmental awareness. We bring our attention to passing thoughts, images, and sensations—maybe a grocery list—and then let the thoughts pass. It can be helpful to listen to instrumental meditation music or follow a guided meditation by a practitioner, which may prompt memories or specific images. If something like a scenario or dream comes to mind, observe it and then reflect on it later.

Focused-attention meditation brings our attention to a particular stimulus, perhaps an object or our breathing. If we get distracted during the meditation, we refocus on the object or our breathing.

Learning to let distracting thoughts pass by helps us avoid pointless thinking when we are not meditating. We become more aware and present, boosting our ability to lead people. Mindfulness practices bring many benefits to organizations. The *Journal of Management* published a study that reviewed more than 4,000 scientific papers. The study investigated how people who completed mindfulness training think, feel, interact, and perform at work. It found that mindfulness helps improve attention, cognition, emotions, behaviour, and physiology. People who completed mindfulness training can focus longer on visual and listening tasks because their attention is more stable and they can stay more focused and present, and less susceptible to distractions from competing demands. Their working memory and information processing also improve. That's because attention becomes efficient when the brain doesn't waste resources on off-task thoughts and actions.

Improving attention through mindfulness and meditation takes consistency. In your organization, you can adopt or share mindfulness training and practices. Simple actions such as being aware of technology devices used in meetings can limit distractions. Choosing what works for you or your organization depends on what resonates. The best thing is to learn from experiences.

For your meditation practice, you might decide to close your eyes and go inward, perhaps by concentrating on your breathing. Or you could focus on an external object to get out of your head. Spend a couple of minutes doing it. With continued practice, increase the frequency and length of time. I start my day with meditation for a few minutes; it's a calming way to experience the morning. During the day, I might meditate for a couple of minutes to refresh my mind. Sometimes, I close my eyes and go inward, or I put on a three-minute instrumental music meditation. You don't have to do anything extravagant—simple techniques work well.

Our attention has the potency to realign ourselves and adjust our focus to the immediate experience. We can free up our attention if we choose to. Being in the moment does more for us than a mind full of clutter.

> **THE BREATHWORK SOLUTION**
>
> I see many people fall into the vacation trap. They deplete themselves and think that on vacation they will get restored. It's false to perceive our holiday as a magic remedy to heal and rejuvenate ourselves. Nurturing our inner state by carving moments to give ourselves attention is best done on a daily basis. We have to break through the cycle of ignoring ourselves and instead nourish ourselves.
>
> An effective way to make space for yourself is breathwork. Inhaling, holding, and exhaling breath goes beyond a

physical experience. The quietness that emerges creates room for inner clarity to surface. I attend a class led by Katrina Malmqvist, an Elemental Rhythm Breathwork Facilitator. Malmqvist often says breath is powerful and free, and you can access it any time.

Before Malmqvist became a practitioner, she separated her corporate and personal life. Like so many of us, Malmqvist used to rush all the time. Once she started doing breathwork, she felt a significant shift: It helped her to slow down, and she found her expectations lowering. This allowed her vision and goals to come into clarity. She began to say no to participating in things that did not resonate for her. Turning inward has enabled Malmqvist to hear her inner voice. She seeks the experience to renew and learn, and this has made her a better leader. She holds space for her team and others to show up and be present.

Breathwork can take a few minutes or as long as you like. One breath sequence goes like this: You inhale through the nose for a count of four, filling up your belly and rolling the breath to expand the lungs. Then you slowly exhale through the mouth, again counting to four. You can repeat this sequence a few times, and it's something you can do whenever you want. Breath helps you to understand your inner state. It stimulates the vagus nerve, which runs from the brain to the large intestine and is a key component of the parasympathetic nervous system. Breathwork helps you to reset. Each breath carries oxygen into your cells. Dropping deeply into the parasympathetic state relaxes the mind and body; for many people, breathwork unlocks emotions, past experiences, or deep-seated beliefs.

> Breathwork is an opportunity to learn and better ourselves. If we do not invest in ourselves, the space becomes filled with mindless activities. To develop practices that support your inner state, be open to peering inside.

PAY ATTENTION TO YOUR INNER STATE

We can only do so many tasks before things start to fall apart. Breaking points vary for everyone, as do the consequences. Depleted patience and feeling fatigued can increase our irritability. We may feel overwhelmed or experience sudden difficulty in making decisions. When we end up in this state, we're not at our best—and it will show. I have been on the receiving end of a leader who snapped and took their frustration out on me. That never feels great. But I've also been on the other side, and even though I didn't raise my voice, I regret that my tone and my facial expression were less than pleasant.

Catching early signs of how we feel alerts our attention to matters that need inquiry. So we must learn to check in with ourselves. The emotions and moods that we function with daily sit at the surface. Then, by going deeper into our inner state, we carry the past and beliefs about the future. We might be aware of what's there, or we might not. But over the years, things like past traumas begin to feel normal, and they can influence our thinking, behaviour, and attitude. These suppressed emotions can emerge at any time. Mental associations tucked far away in our brain end up being triggered, and worries about things that haven't even happened yet might prevent us from understanding what's happening now. A variety of situations hold the potential to stir up disturbing emotions. So, what can we do?

Distracting thoughts can come to mind any time while conversing with colleagues. If we don't brush the thoughts aside, we'll lose focus. It will feel like your mind has escaped to another realm and left your body in the room. In moments like this, feeling our feet on the ground or our body sitting in the chair refocuses attention on the present. Think of the body as an anchor to the experience. A similar concept was in the 2010 film *Inception*, directed by Christopher Nolan. The characters travel through dreams to steal secrets from a person's subconscious. Once in the dream world, the characters can fall into further dimensions of a dream. They call this "a dream within a dream." Getting stuck poses a serious risk, so the characters use an anchor, a physical object that lets them know if they are in the dream world or back in reality.

Luckily, we don't need to carry an object to remind ourselves to be present. When you notice your mind float away, your body remains where you left it. The physical self, in a constant rhythm, interacts with the environment it's in. The body does this through sensory perception. It's how we know what's happening around us. Noticing what we feel physically brings our attention to the nervous system, and we can check in with ourselves about how we feel. Do you sense tension in your body, or do you feel like your usual self? Observing our inner state and surroundings prompts our thinking to slow down. Disrupting ourselves in this way is positive.

Attention to the body draws us out of the mind and the tricks it routinely plays on us. This action helps us regulate our emotions. You may find that you struggle with negative emotions and feelings that repeat. They're hard to stop, and they hijack your cognitive resources. Tuning into yourself often will help you acknowledge what's going on for you. To pull yourself out of a state, ask yourself why you think or behave in certain ways. When you let awareness surface, it can help shift your behaviour and create new habits. It's important to be gentle with yourself by adopting a non-judgmental attitude. You might say to yourself, "There I go again with thoughts of doubt that don't reflect my beliefs." Then, create a statement to reframe how you want to think. Understanding your habitual patterns and spotting them faster lets you adjust your behaviour.

Matea Saule is the founder and owner of Matea Designs, a boutique fashion brand in Melbourne, Australia. When she launched her business, it was about more than fashion. She developed a deeper purpose to help women in Australia and around the world; some company proceeds go toward women's empowerment organizations. This purpose helps her to balance and connect her attention to herself and the present moment.

I asked Saule how she stays present as a leader and brings specific practices into her day. She told me that her daily practice of being present does not follow a particular routine. Instead, she tunes into what she needs that day. And each day, it could be something different. Connecting with nature resonates for her; the outdoors gives her space to observe her thoughts. Saule's core practice involves spending time reading and reflecting, which help her learn different perspectives about life and spiritual growth. Her dedication to expanding herself comes through exploring the art of fashion. With that, Saule

Designs can give more to the world than garments for women. But it all begins with her, and how she manages her inner state.

Building habits to tune into yourself will take practice. It's worthwhile to spend time connecting the body with your thoughts and actions. Engage in activities that capture your attention. Spend time with yourself and enjoy whatever you're doing. Experiences and hobbies that captivate your attention fill the space that otherwise turns into mindless thinking.

If you attempt these changes but still struggle, try observing yourself for a week. Keep a journal handy and jot down distractions, including repetitive mind-wandering. Your notes can help you understand what pulls your attention out of the present. The small actions count. You don't have to go on a yoga retreat. Remember, attention is fragile and vulnerable to stress, poor mood, fear, and a wandering mind. So use your attention wisely.

HOW TO LEAD IN THE PRESENT MOMENT

In today's complex environment, our attention reaches capacity pretty fast. A busy life and never-ending to-do lists put us in a position of bombardment. If you strive to keep your attention consistent and focused all day, you will end up failing. After all, the brain likes to reduce demands to conserve its energy. So give your brain a break, especially when you feel stretched and unable to process information or make decisions. Sometimes, setting your mind free to daydream or think spontaneously helps creativity and problem-solving, as long as you have a positive purpose. Otherwise, you'll just be daydreaming.

It is possible to improve attention span and the ability to focus, but it takes practice and commitment. Here are some helpful tips.

- Begin the day with an intention to be present. Say to yourself that you will be present in the moment. Stating it will help you to remember to bring your attention back when you get distracted.
- Consider the activities you have planned for the day. Prepare yourself to focus on your work and avoid multitasking.
- Get a handle on distractions. Don't respond to emails and text messages as soon as they come in. Silence your phone.
- Spend twenty-five or thirty minutes focused on a task. Doing so boosts your productivity. When you feel good about your actions, your brain reinforces the choices.
- Watch for signs of waning attention, such as if you notice more auditory or visual stimuli. Small thoughts may cross your mind, such as wanting a snack or something to drink; address your need for a break, and then move on.
- Throughout the day, pause for a few seconds to let your mind slow down, shift thoughts, or self-reflect. Taking a few minutes away from an activity helps to realign your attention. Switching tasks to something different also provides relief and new energy to focus.
- Close your eyes. Vision is a critical part of sensory perception. By closing your eyes, you allow the mind to rest.

- Speak with your colleagues without your inner voice judging what they say. You'll notice more, ask better questions, and have a deeper dialogue. It opens your mind to curiosity and improves your ability to understand people's views. A non-judgmental attitude helps you approach problems with acceptance during conflicts. It allows you to move past emotions that can block your thinking from finding a solution.

The message of this chapter? Our attention determines our reality. If we're not focused on the golf ball, on the cycle path, on the trail beneath our feet, we will get distracted. If we're not paying attention to watching where we're going, we're bound to make mistakes. If our concentration is not on what we're doing, our performance suffers. Attention is both fleeting and powerful, so consciously choose to be present in the moment.

When our attention isn't focused, we can get blindsided. Or we fixate on ideas that are based on a false image of reality. That's what happened to Research In Motion, the company behind the Blackberry. Once nicknamed the "Crackberry," the phone with the physical keyboard revolutionized how we receive emails and messaging. It was a huge hit worldwide—until the slick iPhone with its larger glass screen and touch keyboard came to market. RIM's leadership didn't understand the iPhone and its effect on consumers; they saw the product's shortcomings, such as a short battery life and weaker security. They couldn't see the sleek outward beauty and user-friendliness of the iPhone that people worldwide instantly loved. They focused on the

Blackberry's superior engineering, and believed that's what customers wanted. But they got that wrong. Over the course of five years, Blackberry's market value dropped by US $75 billion. At some point over those five years, they should have questioned their version of reality. Yet their path remained unchanged. Their attention was tethered too tightly to their beliefs, and they didn't take the substantial market changes seriously.

> **KEY TAKEAWAYS**
>
> - It's tough to be present throughout the day. Our attention can slip at any moment because a bombardment of stimuli and tasks compete for our attention. When we lose our focus, we may have no idea that we're missing parts of reality. Attempting to multitask only makes matters worse; the quality of our thinking and actions declines when we focus on more than one activity. We're dividing our attention, and that makes us slower to respond and open to making more mistakes.
>
> - A key risk is pushing our attention outside the brain's limits. When that happens, we are prone to making mistakes or forgetting to do something. Half of the brain's capacity gets used up when we speak with another person. When we are talking on the phone while working on our computer, our brain chooses to process only one of these things: the visual information. So we will hear less of what the person is saying.

- For almost 50 percent of our waking hours, we think about something other than what we are doing. Mind-wandering is a typical brain activity. When the mind is not engaged, it occupies itself with more interesting ideas, and thinking becomes repetitive and habitual. Losing attention disconnects us from our actions, making us prone to errors and eroding our perception. We can break wandering thoughts by paying attention to what we are doing in the present moment.

- The voice of our mental chatter likes to note everything that's happening. But all that commentary limits our perception and how we experience reality. We need to turn off the mind's narrator and learn to observe and listen without judging the event or the people we're working with. That helps us to avoid assumptions and gather information critical for a good decision. Needless mental chatter uses up our brain's resources.

- Attention is a precious resource. It directly influences our thoughts and actions, and what we experience. But it's limited. Wherever we place it, that's our understanding of what's happening. Once we hit capacity for attention, we will not be aware of incoming information; the brain will filter it out. We need to pay attention to seeing the whole problem. The ability to do that comes from understanding issues that we can see—the tip of the iceberg—but also looking for things beneath the surface.

- We can improve our attention by focusing on one task at a time and reducing mind-wandering. We can develop new habits that change brain circuits to support our new behaviours. Learn to observe your mind by bringing awareness to what you are doing. Notice your thoughts, and don't get sucked into them. When you lose attention, simply shift it back to the present.

- Mindfulness and meditation produce changes in the brain that reduce mind-wandering. These practices strengthen attention and focus. Mindfulness helps us detect when our attention has slipped. It also improves our ability to regain it and return to our activity. The practice can happen at any time of the day to bring focus to ourselves or our task.

- Pay attention to your inner state. Unchecked emotions strain the brain, cause stress, and reduce our ability to think. A burdened self leads to errors from reduced perception and distracted attention. Tune into yourself and your body to help regulate your emotions. Find the practices that help you connect the body with your thoughts and actions.

- Stay focused in the present, and concentrate with intent on what you're doing. You will succeed in your performance.

Step 2: Become Heart-Centred

Have you ever attended a meeting about an important topic where you ignored a sense or feeling in your stomach? Did you notice it but push it aside? Well, many of us do. We tend not to pay attention to the inner guidance from the heart and gut. We don't receive instruction in business and school about how to understand it. We keep learning the same old frameworks that rely on the rational mind. If an organization teaches emotional intelligence, it's called "soft skills" or described as "touchy-feely." Yet learning to discern and use signals from the heart and gut *is* a skill—period.

So why don't we listen to the signals that flow from the body? In part, it's because mental clutter can throw us off track. For instance, if you're discussing options with your team and the broadcaster in your mind starts talking, it will distract you. You won't notice feelings or sensations in the body. You're too busy listening to the narration. Maybe there is some mind-wandering going on, too. Possibly, you feel bogged down but don't know it. These situations put us in a position to ignore or confuse signals from the heart and gut. Our state of being and what's going on for us influences our ability to notice these signals. The brain does not perform solo when making decisions. Emotion and intuition play a role, too.

Noticing and evaluating the signals from the heart and gut can significantly improve our thinking and decision-making. It enhances our ability to perceive more from ourselves and what's happening around us. So choosing to ignore or doubt our feelings and intuition comes at a cost. We erode the trust that we have with ourselves. This leads to a lack of confidence in our choices that tarnishes our ability to lead effectively.

But when we learn to attune to ourselves, we also can do so with others. In *How to Know a Person*, David Brooks describes getting to know someone as attuning to their rhythms and moods, and gaining a sort of subtle, tacit knowledge that can help us to build connections and trust with people. And that will help us lead effectively. Brooks also argues that we aren't very good at seeing others, or making them feel as if they are seen, heard, and understood. He points out that this is happening "in this age of creeping dehumanization." It's time to change that. Tapping into our emotions and gut feelings isn't irrational. Indeed, doing so actually boosts the quality of our thoughts.

THE HEART BRAIN AND THE GUT BRAIN

Sara Blakely started SPANX in 1998 with US $5,000, and grew the shapeware company to an estimated value of more than $1 billion by 2021. The key to her success was harnessing her intuition. Blakely maintained ownership of the company for a long time, feeling she could not allow outside investors in. (It's still not a public company.) She has said that came from her intuition, and from not wanting to lose her voice. She didn't care about fast growth, and instead wanted to focus on the customer. For 16 years, the company didn't spend money on advertising; it grew from word of mouth. Blakely attributes intuition to running her business and life, calling it an inner knowing. We all possess this ability, but some leaders learn to home in on intelligence that does not come from the mind.

Our decisions are not as rational and deliberate as we like to believe. But how do emotion and intuition play a role? Breakthrough studies reveal that the heart and gut are "little brains." These areas contain complex neural systems—the heart's is called the intrinsic cardiac neural plexus, and the gut's is the enteric neural plexus—that can act independently of the brain. Both regions actively communicate and interact with the body, and are essential to human processes and decision-making.

Dr. J. Andrew Armour, a professor of neurocardiology, came to dub the heart "the heart brain," and that has stuck with others in the field. That's because of extensive research he completed in 1991 that unearthed striking findings. He discovered that the heart's intrinsic nervous system consists of about 40,000 neurons, a complexity that allows the heart to communicate with the brain and body through a few mechanisms: it uses the nervous system, hormones, blood pressure, vibrations created by blood flow, and energy. Not only that, the heart has the capacity to learn and keep its own memories. Following heart transplants, patients have reported inheriting the personality characteristics of their donor. They experience changes in preferences, emotions, identity, and memories from the donor's life. Research shows that cellular memory in the heart transfers causes these changes.

The heart's influence extends beyond our bodies. With an electromagnetic energy field 5,000 times more powerful than the brain's, the heart's energy extends about three feet from our body. A person near us can detect this. You likely have had the experience of being in a meeting and feeling the energy in the room. When discussing a problem, such as a project going wrong, you might have felt stress or tension in the room. Yet other meetings that also focus on a significant problem might have a calmer vibe. Likewise, in a creative discussion about, say, a new product line, the energy in the room can feel upbeat and vibrant, while a similarly positive meeting about innovations might feel flat. That vibe all depends on how people feel, and what they exude in the moment. The experience also applies in one-on-one situations. What we are sensing—if we pay attention—are the signals emanating from someone's heart to their brain and body.

Then there's the gut brain. We all know the gut sends messages to the brain, and the brain responds. For example, the gut alerts us to our needs through physical sensations, such as that growling stomach when we need fuel. Yet it's far more than a gastrointestinal machine that sends out signals when it's time to eat. The gut contains 500 million neurons. It connects to the brain through chemicals, nerves, and the immune system; that's the gut–brain axis. Emotions also create feelings in the stomach—think of that sensation of butterflies when you feel excitement or anticipation. In contrast, nausea can churn in the stomach from worry and anxiety. The body provides us with a continuous stream of information in the form of sensations.

This proven brain–gut connection explains the old adage "trust your gut." Our decisions receive guidance from our gut feelings; we listen to them, and act. At times, the feeling is strong. Have you ever travelled somewhere and, while following directions, sensed that you were going the wrong way? Or, at work, your employees briefed you about an issue, and you got a feeling to not take action? Subtle signals from the gut help us to avoid potential wrong moves. The gut is great at detecting danger but also at acting like an inner compass for intuitive decision-making. Think about a time when you worked on a complex business decision with colleagues. You might have requested lots of data and analysis, yet maybe those numbers had nothing to do with the direction you sensed you should go. Many leaders don't think about how answers come to them; they just sense them. Trusting your gut is understanding these signals and then acting upon them.

Intuition—your heart brain working with your gut brain—plays a vital role in our decision-making. Our intuition can process a lot of information and helps to prevent the mind from becoming overwhelmed. Intuition helps the brain's conscious reasoning because it functions separately and does not take up the conscious brain's resources. The unconscious part of the mind is free to work on problems such as analyzing, comparing, and classifying information. Intuition lightens the load by accessing the different types of knowledge, working through System 1, which is faster. You may recall from "Understanding the Error-Prone Mind" (page 1) that System 1 is the unconscious mind operating on automatic. Let's say you're an executive working on your organization's five-year transformation plan, and final decisions need to happen. You're dealing with a significant amount of information—deliverables, risks, costs, and how to best approach the work. Using your intuition can let your unconscious mind spot patterns and find issues. You might discover understated risks and costs from overconfidence bias. Meanwhile, intuition will also help you surface ideas, insights, and inspiration. You might notice opportunities to approach the work in new ways.

Listening to our intuition makes us more effective at decision-making. Research shows that when we pay attention to our intuition, we get better, faster, and more accurate. We also boost our confidence in what we decide. One study found that coupling nonconscious emotional information with conscious information improves decision-making. The architecture of the brain allows emotional stimuli to be processed quickly, which activates the pathways in the brain that improve decision-making. In other words, intuition works rapidly with the brain to consider our memories, lessons, needs, or preferences. It doesn't require our conscious awareness; we don't have to sit and think things through slowly and deliberately. But we do need to understand the signals coming from the heart and gut. Interpreting these feelings is the means to using heart intelligence.

MIMICKING FACIAL EXPRESSIONS

Stanford and Cornell researchers studied our ability to understand others. Participants' heartbeats and facial expressions were measured when looking at images of people's faces showing fear or disgust. Researchers found that those with a better sense of their bodily sensations could identify the emotions of others.

People incorporate information from their own bodies and use visual input to interpret another person's emotions. We tend to subtly imitate the facial expressions of those we are near. By understanding the cues coming from our own body, we can interpret the emotions of others. Having greater awareness of internal cues enables empathy.

Next time you are in a meeting and are unsure how it's going for people, tune in to your body. Sense what you are feeling along with what you observe. This will lead you to better understand those you are interacting with so you can make better choices when engaging them and steering conversation.

HEART INTELLIGENCE

From the very beginning, Walt Disney set his focus on the customer experience. His advice: "You don't build it for yourself. You know what the people want and you build it for them." Disney would tell his staff to go to the park and watch visitors instead of sitting behind a desk. He wanted his team to stand in line for food, eat lunch at the park, listen to people. Disney himself would watch guests enter the park from the Town Square so he could see their first impressions.

He got it all right. The information that we understand from being in an experience has richness. When the body is physically in an experience it tells us more than we realize. But how? Because of heart intelligence.

Heart intelligence comes from experiences. It's a form of experiential data transmitting from our feelings and sensations. When we interpret this information, it influences our actions, behaviours, and decisions. Recognizing and interpreting what these signals mean leads to insights that inform our perception. Using heart intelligence supports our mental capacity to work on complex problems and think in new ways. We also get better at relating to people and understanding situations.

Knowing how to leverage heart intelligence requires learning to discern information from the heart and gut. We also need to be aware of what can get in the way. It can feel frustrating to sense something but be unable to name it. Two-year-olds often find themselves in this situation. They comprehend what's happening but can't articulate what they think or feel. So, they end up spiralling into distress and feeling frustrated, angry, or sad. But even we grownups can struggle in trying to understand heart intelligence. Misinterpretation also poses a key challenge. We're prone to misreading signals and confusing what's going on. If we do that, we could end up making poor decisions.

The first part of understanding heart intelligence is knowing what's normal for you. Think of it as your regular day-to-day state of being. We can also call it your baseline. Let's say you work in a demanding, high-stress environment. You know your stress tolerance and how to leverage it to increase performance and thrive. People who lack awareness of what feels normal for them make misguided decisions. Many times, I've encountered employees who say that they can work in a high-pressure environment and want a challenge. But once they're in the situation, they crumble; they can't handle the stressful environment and performing activities to meet deadlines. Their inability to understand themselves is, unfortunately, reflected in their decision-making and the results they deliver. These individuals struggle with critical thinking, so understanding any sort of heart intelligence is out of the question for them.

Whatever your normal state of being, it's your baseline. The brain receives several sources of information from the heart and cardiovascular system to establish that baseline. So, if you work in a high-pressure environment and enjoy it, your internal systems regulate to that. The baseline, also called set points, comes from your experiences; how you handle successes and failures and manage daily demands adjusts the set points. Mental and physical processes that link the mind, body, and behaviour maintain stability in your internal world. A sense of security comes from sticking with your established baseline, so when you encounter unfamiliar situations, your internal systems want to return to stability and your state of normal. That's why we resist change.

Let's say you run a line of business and get tasked to work on a large technology transformation project. But that's not the environment you thrive in, since you don't like ambiguity. Well, you will have issues. Your baseline will adjust to one that causes you to feel a lot of stress. Your ability to make decisions will become compromised. Your productivity will also decline, and you will make errors.

If you are unaware of what's affecting your baseline, habitual patterns can form easily. You might react by stress eating, or working more hours even though that's unproductive. Maybe you end up making a big deal of small issues, and snapping at people. Whatever the case, your perception is biased and bends toward your tried-and-true habitual responses. That's how you can get stuck in unhealthy patterns as a leader. So, it's imperative that you build up your capacity to manage your baseline.

> **HOW TO MANAGE YOUR BASELINE**
>
> We need to pay attention to the sensations from emotions, the gut, and the body. Negative feelings bias our perception, and our decisions will come from a place of fear and poor thinking (for example, unclear ideas, distorted understanding, inaccurate conclusions). That makes it easy for the broadcaster in our mind to distract our attention. Not only that, negative feelings lower our mood and throw off our state of normal.
>
> When you spot worry, stress, or fear, take a moment to observe the thoughts that follow. You will gain awareness of what you need to attend to. Empower yourself to adjust your state of being to function more positively.
>
> Some ways that you can become more aware of your baseline follow.
> - If you have a day when you feel off, or your patience is wearing thin, ask yourself what's going on. You might answer "I feel frustrated" or "Something is bothering me." You will have to consider the underlying cause of the emotion so that you can move out of it.

- If you notice you're feeling a sense of distrust toward your colleagues or employees, question why. Behind those feelings are ideas and perceptions that have formed from experiences. So you want to unearth the instances that have led you to those feelings. By bringing awareness, you will identify the bias.

- If you get a feeling that a situation is bad, such as a new product idea or shifting the company's strategy, start questioning your thinking. It could be that the fear or worry is stemming from a past experience that you think will repeat, or maybe there are too many unknowns. Tuning into the emotion is the first step in accepting what's happening. Next, think about considering ideas from new perspectives to change your views.

Openness to learning and experiencing new situations can help us shift our thought patterns. These opportunities help us move away from habitual ways of perceiving. Our set points can evolve if we have awareness of the responses that we want to change. We can move to a new state of normal. These experiences create a type of implicit memory that will help shape our perception going forward. We can then better manage our feelings and behaviour in situations, and not react impulsively. If we don't take any action, we become prone to old thinking patterns and filters.

Staying in tune with our emotions helps us to gauge our baseline, allowing us to adjust it. When we increase our internal awareness, it improves not only how well we understand ourselves but also others.

The second part of understanding heart intelligence is about recognizing the signals. We need to notice them and evaluate their meaning. The heart sends more neural information to the brain than the brain sends to the heart. The brain receives information about our emotions and then takes action. For example, if we feel short-term or chronic stress, the brain will respond by triggering a response in the body. Stress hormones get released, which then constrict blood vessels and increase blood pressure. The heart then starts working harder; heart rate increases, requiring more oxygen.

The body is always alerting us to its needs. If we feel cold, we put on a sweater. If we feel hungry, we have a snack. Information flowing from emotions also affect the body. For instance, a stomach flutter, tense muscles, dry mouth, or a racing heart bring our attention to physical needs. Maybe the cause is an upcoming product launch or some other deliverable we're nervous about. Whenever we feel these signals, we need to self-inquire.

Getting comfortable with the continuous practice of turning inward is fundamental to understanding what we sense or feel. It takes practice, however, so be patient. When we notice a feeling or sensation, even for a quick second, we need to let it emerge, because if we dismiss it too quickly by telling ourselves it's nothing, we're suppressing our heart intelligence. In *How to Know a Person*, David Brooks calls heart intelligence "one of the greatest miracles in all nature." He says the voice is trying to make sense of events we experience by creating a story with coherence, meaning, and purpose.

But how do we know if our inner voice isn't just mental chatter, that broadcaster inside your head?

We can differentiate between the two by paying attention to our body and feelings. Do you feel yourself contracting or expanding? The body contracts when it's tense, anxious, or worried. Feelings that come from fear also cause symptoms such as shallow breathing, or we might close up and cross our arms or lean away from people in conversations. The thoughts that follow will sound critical, judgmental, negative, or worrisome. That's the broadcaster at work. Yet, when our inner voice speaks, when our feelings come from intuition, the body feels good. We feel a sense of ease, contentment, or excitement. We feel creative and can see things from different perspectives. New ideas come to mind with little effort. Our thoughts guide us to a choice that *feels natural*. We might say to ourselves, "This feels right."

The consistent practice of listening to signals creates a stronger connection to our intuition. But the caveat is that the mind must be free of mental chatter. So, being present is crucial. The other challenge is accessing heart intelligence without unpleasant emotions getting in the way. Research about stress and emotions shows that negative mood blocks intuition when making decisions. If negative mood and stress start to feel like a normal part of yourself, you will not notice emotions that can muddle your thinking, nor will you catch how they affect your behaviour. Learning how and when to regulate your emotions is important to working with heart intelligence. When something is off balance with your normal state, your attention will be prompted by a physical sensation or a feeling, and receiving that signal is a good thing. Because once you notice, you can do something about it.

TRIAL AND ERROR

If your heart and gut are sending you signals, you might wonder if you can trust them. But with practice you'll build up your ability to read and interpret heart intelligence. In *How to Know a Person*, David Brooks points out findings from neuroscientist Lisa Feldman Barrett: We believe what we see and hear influences our feelings, but it's actually the other way around. What we feel influences our sight and hearing. So if we increase our understanding of heart intelligence, we can then perceive and understand how we experience reality and act accordingly.

You can start out by testing low-risk decisions and, in time, tackle bigger ones. To prepare, first notice whether you have mental chatter in your head. If not, has your mind wandered? Have you had difficulty focusing your attention? Ensuring your mind is clear will help you to turn inward and let your inner voice emerge. And that removes some of the guess work.

Then, test your heart intelligence with small questions during your daily activities. For example:

- At dinnertime, ask yourself what you feel like eating. Whatever comes to you first, go with it. You're listening to what your body craves. If you decide by listening only to your mind, you might go with your diet plan or something you know is already prepared. Afterward, you'll notice that even though you finished the food, you don't feel content.

- When you are about to relax in the evening in front of the TV, ask yourself what you feel like watching. Decide on the kind of entertainment you want to experience based on your mood. If you follow your mind, you will likely watch the series you're in the middle of because your mind knows it's logical to finish what you've already started.

These are just two examples of how we use heart intelligence in our day-to-day that we don't tend to notice. By being intentional, however, you can test out heart intelligence in these low-risk experiences. When you feel ready, move on to bigger decisions. For example:

- Consider your work schedule for the week. Have a look at your calendar and think about what you have underway. Listen to yourself: pay attention to what thoughts and emotions arise, and what you feel you should work on rather than simply following the chronological order of your calendar. You might then choose an item that you fully engage and flow with. You may become more productive and faster at your work because your heart and body are aligned to do it.

- When you meet with an employee for a one-on-one meeting or a coaching session to help them with their work, tune in to yourself. Let your employee know beforehand that you're testing out a new practice. As you listen to your employee talk about a challenge they're dealing with, or give updates on how their work is going, follow your intuition about what questions to ask. Listen to your instinct and be willing to veer away from the planned questions you typically ask. Let these thoughts flow seamlessly into your mind. You'll notice the questions are open and focus on your employee's

> experience. It's a positive sign if your employee comes up with insights and conclusions that support their learning and progress.
>
> During these practices, you might misread signals and make mistakes. But remember, it's all learning, and you'll be better off in the long run. Intuition comes from experience, so the more you practice with new experiences, the more you will help your unconscious processes work with your conscious mind.

AVOID THE INFLUENCE OF NEGATIVE EMOTIONS

It's one thing to have an off day and realize that you aren't in the best spirits. As we've seen, regulating our emotions and moving out those feelings is critical to understanding heart intelligence. But what if those bad emotions are chronic? What can we do to stop ourselves from acting upon them and making terrible decisions?

Emotions can bias perception and shape what we think. For instance, if you experience anxiety all the time, unnecessary worries can cloud your mind. The anxious feeling in your stomach can disrupt your thought process and discourage taking risks that could be good for business. You might be fed up with life and feel pessimistic, which could lead you to view ideas for innovation or new opportunities as a waste of time. To resolve it, you need to self-reflect. Sometimes negative emotions result from biases lodged deep in our mind—for example, sexism or racism. Those ideas came from somewhere, and we attached negative feelings to them. So we need to unravel those beliefs and set a new reality by practising the following.

1. Look at the situation and evaluate your response. Is it clear what's driving your thoughts and feelings? Identify and name your views and feelings. Bring awareness to what's there with acceptance and nonjudgment. Ingrained perceptions trigger unpleasant emotions such as frustration, anger, sadness, and anxiety, and should prompt self-regulation.

2. Reconsider the context again and evaluate the situation. Try to bring in different sources of information and data, and seek other's opinions. Ask others to share their thought processes, and then try to think through the perspectives they shared. By doing so, you're practising using empathy to understand the logic.

3. Reframe the situation by applying what you learned.

Repeating these steps will help expand how you think. Keep in mind that whenever we have strong feelings, whether positive or negative, it tunnels our vision. Don't jump to conclusions. Instead, slow down your thinking when you spot the chronic negative emotion arising.

HEART-CENTRED LEADERSHIP

In 2014, the U.S. Office of Naval Research embarked on a four-year study on intuition and premonition. It wanted to figure out how sailors and marines could use their "Spidey senses." The research program studied intuitive decision-making, memory, and perception, looking at how to enhance those elements through implicit learning.

The intent was to improve the ability of personnel to make split-second decisions and inform future operations related to cyberspace and unmanned systems. Yet the Navy knew gut instinct develops through experience. So, they wanted to understand the intuitive decision-making process—and how people could gain experience over the course of days rather than years. These scenarios weren't just about the equipment but new skills for personnel to harness for decisions. This insight would help them create a new set of training practices to enhance performance in the field. The findings of the study weren't publicly disclosed, but according to one report, the ensuing program that's now offered in the Navy enables marines' situational awareness and is referred to as "sensemaking."

Increasing your ability to use heart intelligence in the workplace comes down to experience. The Navy was right about that. Instinct comes from situations we go through that develop our intuition. But you don't have to recreate the battlefield. Like Walt Disney, put yourself in the experiences of your business, rather than looking at it from afar (see page 67). Herb Kelleher, founder and former CEO of Southwest Airlines, succeeded in his purpose to "democratize the skies" by making travel affordable for the average American. His methods were unconventional and set high standards for customer service. Kelleher regularly boarded flights to observe the experience of passengers. He also implemented a 15-minute turnaround at the gates to get the plane back in the air by encouraging flight crews to help clear and service the aircraft. Kelleher put employees and customers first. He knew the key to success was in experiences and understanding the business deeply in order to guide complex decisions.

Practising heart intelligence in decisions offers a great opportunity to build up your experience. To get started, make sure to get out of your head. If you're in a discussion with your colleagues, don't only look at analysis and numbers to make decisions. Instead, ask a few questions to prompt dialogue. Let's say you're meeting with the executive team to discuss budget cuts. You can easily get caught in focusing on the bottom line and numbers that you've been given. Consider the following: What do we observe? What does this mean? How do I feel? What do I sense? What will we gain, and what will we lose? How will our decisions impact employees and customers in the short and long term?

Simple yet powerful questions will help your heart and gut signals to start communicating. Pay attention and share what you think and feel. Encourage your colleagues to do so as well. You will find that you have greater insight to what exists behind the numbers, and that will help you to make the best decisions for today and the future. Questions such as these also encourage empathy and compassion. But only if you're open to it.

Empathy and compassion support our ability to collaborate, think through different perspectives, and develop new ideas. When we feel empathy, we get to know the emotions of others. We can transport ourselves into others' experience by listening with openness.

With practice, you can raise your awareness to notice signals and understand information coming from heart intelligence. Pay attention by observing the experience rather than judging it. Use your intuition to engage in the conversation. Sensing what's happening in the moment lets you adjust your communication.

Tackling challenges when emotions run high and all over the place makes things difficult for everyone involved. It's worse when people have limited self-awareness. It leads to unproductive conversations, and wasted energy and time. But you can use your heart intelligence to help you navigate the conversation. Just as you would bring awareness to the emotions that affect your perception and reactions, you do the same for the group. You bring awareness to what's going on to help people shift the conversation. In *How to Know a Person*, David Brooks calls emotions "mental faculties that help you steer"—meaning emotions help you adjust to different situations.

When we pay attention to the experience of others, we change how we relate and interact. We find ways to work better with people through empathy and compassion. Empathy carries information about emotions, while compassion prompts action in response to those feelings. We can think more acutely about the needs of employees, customers, suppliers, and other stakeholders. These views represent parts of reality that we can't see or understand. How one person perceives the world is different from how everyone else perceives it. By opening up these perspectives, we can find innovation and opportunities, and solve challenges in new ways. Empathy and compassion help us to push thinking outside the traditional realm.

HEART-CENTRED INNOVATION

In 2023, I sailed with Virgin Voyages to the Caribbean. During the trip, I went on an excursion to a local women's co-op in Puerto Plata, Dominican Republic. The co-op transforms paper into items like notebook covers and jewellery. The social enterprise helps women and girls with their livelihoods and teaches them new skills. Virgin Voyages offers experiences like this to positively impact people's lives. I spoke with Jill Stoneberg, Senior Director of Social Impact and Sustainability at Virgin Voyages. She said the intent behind these experiences is three-pronged: 1) They want to offer authentic experiences to their guests. 2) They want to promote sustainable tourism as an integral part of their business. 3) They have an impetus to work with local entrepreneurs so that communities thrive. These actions support their vision and purpose: "Create an epic sea-change for all." Their "all" includes guests, crew, partners, communities, and the ocean. They consider these stakeholders at the centre of their decisions and actions.

Virgin Voyages' vision and purpose influence everything they do. Coupling that with creativity helps them design innovative experiences for guests. The itineraries, planned with great detail, encourage wellness and fun, including responsible travel. Virgin Voyages advocates for sustainability and demonstrating its commitments. The cruise business has a reputation for extracting and taking, but Virgin Voyages does not want to be the ship that takes. So, they ask themselves how they will create a sea change for the community. They consider that when developing and managing their community excursions. Virgin Voyages expects its tour operators to meet the Global Sustainable Tourism Council standards. With those expectations comes support to help their partners along the way. Virgin Voyages is serious about keeping people as its focal point. Its willingness to be open and welcome new ideas focuses on connecting with people's hearts and minds.

Heart-centred leadership creates value that expands and grows further. The inspiration can support innovation, like Virgin Voyages, or help solve problems in new ways. A leader who is doing that is Patrice Sulton, founder of DC Justice Lab in Washington, D.C., a non-profit launched in 2020. DC Justice Lab advocates, researches, and organizes large changes to the District of Columbia's criminal and legal system. Sulton helped run the decade-long project revising the city's outdated Criminal Code. After operating for a year, DC Justice Lab was actively supporting three sets of recommendations authored by Sulton. The scope included overhauling the Criminal Code to transform policing in the city. D.C. Council endorsed the revised code. But, once the review reached Congress, it was blocked from becoming law.

DC Justice Lab works with residents affected by the legal system. Its work has led to several local policies and programs approved by the District—for example, a pilot project to divert 25 percent of mental health calls to specialists rather than police. Also, it drafted policies to decriminalize street vending, and collaborated with others to decrease gun violence and guide the creation of new policies. It wrote several bills introduced by lawmakers, such as banning solitary confinement in local jails, and ensuring children receive protection during searches and interrogations. A couple of years after implementation, these accomplishments began to create robust change for society. What sets DC Justice Lab apart is its compassion. That inspires its distinct approach and values.

DC Justice Lab echoes the message that community violence cannot have a resolution if met with state violence. Using force—policing, prosecution, and punishment—will not create long-term change. The organization feels it's imperative to lead with compassion when interacting with stakeholders, and considers the experience of each person affected by the potential law change. After identifying positive or negative changes, the goal is to achieve balance for all. Patrice and her team maintain connections with people in the community, and invite them into a shared space for dialogue. The conversation with stakeholders goes deep with empathy and compassion to understand the complexity and impacts on community safety. The insights help inform extensive research to support policy changes.

At times, DC Justice Lab might not know the best course of action. But the people behind it trust the objective to be right by sensing how they feel. To help her team, Patrice uses role-playing to illustrate compassion. She demonstrates asking questions to get to the *why*, and encourages her team to have confidence in their choices. Patrice empowers them with the message that caring matters and that the world can use more of it. She tells her team that if the work gets the community out of violence, then go for it. DC Justice Lab will continue its momentum to create societal change.

As you can see, it is possible to find ways to create change by leading with our hearts and trusting our intuition. These heart-centred approaches can result in healthier personal lives, healthier organizations—and even a healthier society.

KEY TAKEAWAYS

- Feelings and intuition create the conscious experience of how we perceive ourselves and the world around us. We need to pay attention to the signals that come from the heart and the gut—it's a skill. Emotions and intuition, along with cognition, play a critical role in decision-making.

- The heart and gut are "little brains." The heart's intrinsic nervous system consists of about 40,000 neurons, and communicates with the brain and body. The gut contains 500 million neurons, and influences information processing. It alerts our attention to needs through physical sensations and emotions.

- Intuition comes from various sources, including instinct, subconscious knowledge, embodied cognition, and insights based on experience. Intuition is vital for decision-making and prevents the mind from getting overwhelmed. Listening to our intuition enhances the quality, speed, and accuracy of our decision-making.

- Heart intelligence is a form of data that comes from experiences. Learning to interpret heart intelligence is crucial, and to detect it, we need to know our normal state of being. That helps distinguish heart intelligence from mental clutter. So, managing our inner state and regulating our emotions is necessary to understanding heart intelligence.

- When you notice a feeling or sensation, bring your attention to it. Pay attention to quick thoughts that cross your mind as well. Evaluating the signals requires discerning our inner voice from the narrator in our head. A simple way to decipher is to notice whether you feel yourself contracting or expanding. Fear, which usually comes from that inner broadcaster, makes you feel tense, anxious, or worried. But the inner voice from heart intelligence feels good. You feel ease, contentment, or excitement. That inner voice guides you to a natural choice.

- We need to be aware of chronic negative emotions that can affect our thinking and decisions. Self-reflect to find the deep hidden beliefs that bias your perception. Re-evaluate situations with information, data, and the perspective of others to help reframe your thinking.

- Improving our ability to use heart intelligence comes from experiences. Put yourself in experiences to observe and make sense of what's happening. Also, bring heart intelligence into decision-making. Ask yourself, What do I observe? What does this mean? How do I feel? What do I sense?

- Empathy and compassion help us to collaborate, think through different perspectives, and develop new ideas. Empathy carries information about emotions, while compassion prompts action in response to those feelings. Understanding the experience of others changes how we perceive, relate, and interact with others. Reflecting through others allows us to see parts of reality that we can't see or understand. By increasing our perception, we can discover innovation, opportunities, and new ways to solve challenges.

Step 3: Stay Interconnected

I call it the illusion of separateness: We see ourselves as individuals rather than connected with one another. We don't think about how our distinct consciousness—our identity—relates to the collective consciousness of humanity. We assume our thoughts and actions impact only us, and that we can choose when we influence others. Yet every action we take *does* affect others—and failing to see that leads us to make self-interested, biased decisions in isolation.

The influential psychoanalyst Eric Erikson described identity as a "fundamental organizing principle which develops constantly throughout the lifespan." His popular theory on the development of self-identity defined eight stages: infancy, early childhood, pre-school, school age, adolescence, young adulthood, middle adulthood, and maturity. Along the way we deal with conflict, and if we handle it successfully, our sense of self grows. Erikson believed that social interactions and relationships influence the development of self.

So if relational factors play a key role in our identity, why do we get caught up in perceiving ourselves as separate? Because the social constructs around us, including school and the workplace, promote that separateness. These environments encourage individualistic behaviour. We end up defining ourselves by our age, background, ethnicity, occupation, and so on. We put these labels on ourselves because we have a need for social belonging—and that's what everyone else is doing. Think about it: In the very early years of life we learn to acknowledge our existence by saying our name and "me." Then we arrive in school, and for many years focus on individual learning. We develop behaviours and habits that link our actions with receiving a reward, whether that's a grade or some form of recognition. The performance evaluation carries on as we progress into workplace environments. We get graded again, but now we have pay and performance bonuses attached. The pattern of performing as an individual and creating outcomes for ourselves is deeply etched into our minds. Yet, we don't realize that defining ourselves in these ways limits the way we understand our inner state.

Some organizations have adopted practices to incentivize shared goals and team performance. While that's helpful, it does not undo what the brain has learned over the course of our lives. We are taught to value individual achievement. We have personal goals and learn concepts such as "live your best life." It's as if we exist in our own world. Over the past couple of decades, social media has reinforced this belief; getting likes and creating viral posts appeal to the desires of the ego for status, competition, and superiority. (On top of that, the behaviour is greatly incentivized; influencers make their living off pointing the camera at themselves.) These ideas seep into our consciousness and shape how we see ourselves. The notion of separateness is ingrained, accepted without question.

On the surface, the focus on "me" may sound like a good thing. But it does not nurture the inner state, and so it disconnects us from ourselves and everything that extends beyond us. This illusion of separateness means we are missing what's happening outside our own individual existence. We need to bring our awareness to those things if we are to change our perception.

If we cannot notice a world outside of our own,
then we fail to understand the implications.

MAKE DECISIONS OUTSIDE OF YOURSELF

The decisions that you make in life are about *you*, of course. But you lose sight of decisions and consequences when you see yourself as distinct, because in fact your choices affect everyone around you. If you accept a new leadership opportunity, it's not only going to affect your personal life, it has implications that extend outward. What will you do with that leadership opportunity? What results will you achieve, for whom, and why?

The answers go beyond your team and company, and into the wider world. What you choose to focus on will influence your decisions and actions. Beware of making decisions based upon *your* beliefs and how *you* think, because putting your agenda above the organization's is not good decision-making, even if you think your intentions are coming from a good place. Instead, consider others so that you challenge your thinking to expand it. That will lead you to richer insights, better ideas, and stronger decision-making.

When I was VP of Payments at a financial institution, I was leading a major credit card system transformation. Meanwhile, the digital team reached out to ask for my approval to deploy some new digital capabilities for customers. There was a risk this could affect the credit card system implementation, so I was reluctant. I could feel resistance in my stomach. After all, the payments business was a key revenue provider and a bigger book of business. I thought my instinct to safeguard against risks was in the best interest of the organization. But then I realized it was fear that was shaping my perception. So when the digital team came back with a strong risk mitigation plan, I said yes. Everything went well, and we all gained new insights about coordinating concurrent IT changes.

Assuming that our own agenda is the most important will bias our decision-making, but we also need to watch out for behaviours that make us less likely to help colleagues in need. The "It's not my problem" attitude is not helpful when so many decisions happen daily. We get so caught up with busy-ness that we are like hamsters on a wheel, so it's natural to put up some barriers to protect ourselves from drowning in work. Siloed teams are encouraged, and people will focus on their piece of the puzzle. But who is thinking about the bigger picture to guide decisions?

Unfortunately, lower performance, more errors, and less innovation result when people can't see connections between their work. People tend to duplicate work, make assumptions, and ignore critical information from other teams. Leaders can also fall victim to drawing boxes around what they think decisions affect. Cherry picking information to consider when making a decision means there are other factors being left out. Avoiding "analysis paralysis" for the sake of simplifying a decision is arbitrarily putting a fence around decisions. It creates false perceptions. Because all the things we avoid are still there.

> **ASK FOR OPINIONS**
>
> Remember, we really see only a fraction of what's happening, so seeking the opinions of others provides insight into what we don't notice. Here are a few ways that leaders can actively encourage people to share their thoughts. The critical skill you are practising is listening to others. Because when you do, you notice a world outside of your own.
>
> - At the outset of discussions, set the tone for the type of participation that will help the conversation.
> - You can facilitate the dialogue so that you don't have one or two voices dominating the conversation; call on those who sit quietly.
> - Before you start working on a project, issue, or solution, consider the sources of information that will expand your perspective. Speak with people who can provide counsel, challenge your thoughts, or support your outcomes.

If we rely upon only our observations and don't seek those of others, we can misconstrue our own views as facts and create a false reality. This limited perspective only strengthens our illusion of separateness, and a growing disconnect emerges between how we perceive our actions and their consequences. In 2018, Pacific Gas & Electric (PG&E), the California natural gas and electricity provider, pleaded guilty to 84 counts of manslaughter and was placed under criminal probation for five years after its poorly maintained power grid caused a fire that destroyed the town of Paradise. Even during the company's probation, which ended in early 2022, it was responsible for 31 wildfires that killed 113 people, burned nearly 1.5 million acres, and destroyed some 24,000 structures. The company knew the risks of not updating its infrastructure—maintaining its powerlines and replacing aging equipment—yet didn't connect that risk with taking action to mitigate the danger. The judge wrote that systemic problems at PG&E remain entrenched.

WE'RE NOT ALONE

Shared mental models, explicit or implicit, can enter your organization from the mainstream. These beliefs come across as how the world works. Take, for example, shareholder primacy. "The sole purpose of a business is to generate profits for its shareholders." The statement appeared in a 1970s *Time* magazine piece. The op-ed from a prominent 20th-century economist, Milton Friedman, had a profound influence globally. He conveyed the belief that generating value puts shareholders at the core. That view became the predominant force behind business models and how to operate.

Fifty-plus years later, we need to rethink whether this belief system makes sense. Shareholder primacy encourages lines and boundaries between people, entities, and nature. These beliefs produce a transactional and linear approach to running organizations. This touches everything that we do, and it influences how our teams work, and how we innovate and interact with one another. It also affects the way we consider the external environment and engage our stakeholders.

The problem with shareholder primacy is that it fails to consider the complexity of today's world. Leaders who care only about shareholder value ignore the impact this has on everyone else. What's more, when we look at value creation from a purely financial lens, it closes off possibilities that could be beneficial for the company. Yet, value creation exists beyond the economic dimension if we choose to see it that way. We can produce non-monetary benefits for people, communities, and the natural environment.

In the 2014 book *Firms of Endearment: How World-Class Companies Profit from Passion and Purpose* by Raj Sisodia et al., a research study looked at companies that do more. Publicly traded companies in the assessment included Southwest Airlines, UPS, Starbucks, and Whole Foods. These companies outperformed the S&P 500 by 14 times over a period of 15 years. The organizations brought a common focus to customers, employees, suppliers, shareholders, and communities. The companies care about what they do and the impact of their decisions. As a result, their choices create value beyond the singular financial dimension. Shared mental models can work for us when designed with intent.

Like people, entities have identities. A company's brand and mission give purpose to the goods and services it provides to the world. Yet, unlike human beings, entities can outlive us. All that makes up an organization remains until someone changes it. The ideas that have been instilled about whom the organization creates value for, and why, are tough to change because the illusion of separateness seeps in too easily. Naturally a business's industry and its sector create lines and boundaries, influencing how it operates. But the beliefs of its leadership are the core drivers of value creation. If leaders strive to serve one stakeholder—the shareholders—they end up ignoring others. Operating with these blinders on warps perception and attention. Leaders are less likely to identify, acknowledge, and consider all of the impacts of their actions and decisions. Leaving a trail of harm damages brand reputation and diminishes the potential to create value. But there's also the moral question of existing only to turn a profit—an unsustainable and uninspiring way to the future. Eventually your employees, customers, and other stakeholders will come to an opinion about you. If it's bad, you and your business will lose.

SHARED ASSUMPTIONS

It's far better to for leaders to ensure there is a common understanding of shared assumptions, beliefs, and behaviour. What we believe about value creation and the impacts of our actions will be mirrored in our teams. Our attitude toward what matters replicates in the behaviours of our employees. Consistency, an underrated virtue of team performance, can act as a catalyst. People can spot the reasons for decisions and know what to expect when they work with different teams. Taking the guesswork out reduces errors and frees up people's capacity to put more effort into work that matters.

But harnessing this type of collective energy in an organization requires connection. Connection among people flourishes when there's clarity about shared assumptions, beliefs, and behaviours. The consistency of behaviour that results builds trust among employees and better working relationships—people know they can count on colleagues and vice versa. Healthy team interactions lead to less waste, more productivity, and increased engagement.

Establishing true understanding across the organization will yield continuous benefits. While communicating what the company's vision and goals are is standard practice, that doesn't go deep enough. A company's assumptions, beliefs, and behaviours make up the mental model that drives that company's activities, and if that mental model is explicit—if teams share those assumptions, beliefs, and behaviours—then collaboration and communication flow easier because people know what to expect. Organizations can create an explicit mental model by defining their beliefs and ways of working. Describing what's so important about working together, what outcomes you want to achieve, and why, enables people to really think and to find creative solutions. It fosters alignment within and across teams, with synergies that make way for smoother coordination of work.

But if an organization has a mental model that is implicit, and its assumptions, beliefs, and behaviours are not clearly defined, it can have the opposite effect. It's challenging to provide guidance to people when we don't know what's driving their thoughts and behaviours. It's difficult to lead change when we can't see the mental starting point. Team members are confused and disjointed, they're not working together in alignment, and their decisions are slow, sloppy, and prone to conflict. If we don't share thinking, people make assumptions they think are right, and the implementation of any change will face many obstacles. Communication and change strategies go to waste because of the inability to understand the invisible.

So a keen awareness of the mental models in an organization is vital for the future; without that awareness, we are in the dark about what shared mental models prevail. Creating organizational change gets complicated when people rely on their default beliefs. Finding the common beliefs and assumptions in an organization requires effort. Identifying and setting shared mental models is not a one-time activity but an ongoing dialogue. Learning to use transparency and stating explicit assumptions supports conscious choices. We need to identify the kind of beliefs team members hold that could block new ideas. To do that, we need to encourage individuals to share how they arrived at their conclusions. When they share their story, we can understand the beliefs that they hold and the journey that led them to make assumptions. Conversations such as these not only help us as leaders but also help employees gain self-awareness about their thought processes. They can identify the ideas they felt clear about and those they ended up making assumptions for. Bit by bit, people's thinking will shift into greater alignment as a collective organization.

BEWARE THE C-SUITE DISCONNECT

How do you know if your organization is being held back by implicit mental models? By taking a good hard look at the assumptions touted by senior leaders and those of front-line employees. I spoke with Claudia Baerwolff, Director of Strategy at a multinational engineering and construction company. Companies operating in these traditional sectors—e.g., natural resources and industrial construction—must play a big role in reaching net-zero climate targets.

I asked Baerwolff for her observations about shared beliefs and creating transformation for that kind of company. She said that the beliefs of large organizations in traditional industries with established core values are embedded in everything that they do: in the hierarchy, work practices, incentives, and so on. Yet those core beliefs seem to differ from those at the top. There is an absence of interconnectedness: The C-suite may be setting new strategic values such as net-zero and decarbonization—but those values don't go beyond that level; they're not executed on the front lines. The result? A growing disconnect of what are supposed to be shared assumptions between the top of those organizations and their functional areas. The pursuit of new strategic goals fails to gain traction because the thinking does not align—and so core beliefs and new strategic ones remain separate things. When leaders don't see the misaligned assumptions, it muddles not only their thinking but everyone else's in the organization. Execution only gets harder.

WHO DO YOU AFFECT?

You need to know who and what you affect, both directly and indirectly. Developing this understanding happens when you observe connections and relationships. People and organizations don't function in isolation from the world. Peter Senge, author and Senior Lecturer at MIT, in *The Fifth Discipline*, states that we must see ourselves in the systems we are part of. Senge advocates for systems thinking to observe and understand the whole. He's right. Only looking at the parts doesn't allow perception of what else exists. We need to identify the holistic space in which organizations operate. We have to change our behaviour to appreciate and understand the interconnectedness surrounding us. Only when we identify connections can we know the relationship of our thoughts and actions and what ends up in the world.

Consider how an ecosystem works. The planet demonstrates the balance of interconnectedness in living nature and biodiverse systems. The intricacy of these systems has a complexity that sometimes flows in harmony or spirals into chaos. All species within the ecosystem affect the nature of it. Then, as that ecosystem changes, everything it consists of evolves, and the cascading effect allows the system to self-heal or deteriorate. That effect showcases a deep reliance on connection—just like your organization's connection with the world outside of it. Harmony can return as long the system hasn't degraded to the point of erosion. Nature holds lessons that we can draw upon. We can reflect on the ripple effect of our words and actions. Those effects aggregate inside the organization among its people, and extend to stakeholders and even the planet. The starting point requires awareness of the connections and relationships your organization touches.

To see these connections more clearly, we need bring in people who can help us uncover missed perspectives. That's not easy. A research study found that we empathize with people in our "in-group." Those not considered in our in-group get left out of empathetic responses. And we need those people in order to get a good view of a highly complex environment.

We need to make an effort to notice the relationships around us, and see how our beliefs, decisions, and actions affect them. We need to appreciate that we're part of something bigger, and that awareness gives meaning to how we contribute to experiences beyond ourselves. Feeling connected to the external environment *starts from within*. Then, what happens in the external environment comes back to *reflect within us*.

Developing awareness of the ecosystems we take part in takes openness and curiosity. People perceive in different ways. Building a visual representation can help because it's easier to spot connections and see patterns. Creating a diagram of the ecosystem can become common ground for testing assumptions. We can identify implicit beliefs, subjective interpretations, and biases. Discussing what people observe is an opportunity to make discoveries in the moment.

I led the strategy and transformation planning when Citizens Bank of Canada became Vancity Community Investment Bank. During that time, my team and I set out to understand the social finance market in Canada. It was tough to find information and make sense of it; the Canadian market looked fragmented, with activities scattered across the country. As we dove in, I got my team to start plotting whatever we unearthed onto a whiteboard. We spoke with stakeholders across the country, people from government, finance providers, community organizations, non-profits, and social enterprises.

After our board filled up, we transposed the information into a digital format connecting relationships between parties. Then one day, we spotted some patterns. We discovered a cluster of social impact activities in the Greater Toronto Area, the Maritimes, and Alberta. These were regional ecosystems operating organically that functioned as part of the overall Canadian market. By looking at a scattered market, our discoveries led to opportunities that would otherwise have remained outside of our perception. There's something quite meaningful about the game we learn to play as children, "I spy with my little eye..."

PRACTISING INTERCONNECTEDNESS

We can practise interconnectedness in decision-making, engaging with stakeholders, innovation, and finding opportunities. We can learn to think about others when we make decisions. It's helpful to embed these behaviours in the decision-making process. Yet we won't succeed if it's only the executive team that follows this approach. It needs to be practised throughout an organization. Exploring the impacts of decisions works best in open and transparent conversations. And people learn better when working together.

We can use the decision-making process as a tool to expand awareness across an organization and help to broaden people's perceptions. New thinking will come from perspectives that we access from connecting ideas. The actions that come out of that exercise provide an experience to reflect upon. Ask your teams how the decision-making process went, if they have any key insights, and how they feel about the outcomes. The knowledge that your organization gains from it increases the understanding of interconnectedness.

Possibilities open up when we decide to bring attention outside of boundaries. But none of this is possible if we don't try to identify the impacts of decisions on others. This also means we must become more open to learning about the experiences of others.

NESTLÉ'S EXTERNAL COUNCIL

Engaging with stakeholders is an important way to broaden perspective. Nestlé, a multinational food and drink conglomerate, uses a comprehensive stakeholder approach. Since 2009, Nestlé has worked with an external council that advises its executive board. The council is a large, diverse global stakeholder network that helps the company set strategic priorities and support its reporting and disclosure process, and provides input on the strategy's long-term sustainability and social and economic impact.

Nestlé's network of stakeholders includes those affected by their operations and groups that influence what they do. Together, they discuss topics such as climate change, nutrition, and sustainable sourcing. These conversations help

> Nestlé's teams develop new capabilities and enable them to take collective action.
>
> Gathering perspectives and feedback from stakeholders improves what we do. We will learn something important and build better relationships with those that influence success.

Interacting with stakeholders continuously moves us away from transactional relationships. Changing the passive connection to an active one creates new sources of innovation. Banca Etica, a cooperative bank in Italy and Spain, has deep connections with its community. They use principles of ethical finance to guide what they do. The bank funds projects that support well-being, the social economy, sustainability, and international cooperation. Banca Etica operates 90 groups of volunteer members called Territorial Initiative Groups (TIGs). The TIGs work in local districts, elected by the bank's members, and hold sessions with members to elicit their feedback. New ideas and innovations arise that Banca Etica can act upon. The TIGs also help build relationships with the social economy. They support the credit adjudication process.

The standard practice for banks is to keep the process in internal channels, but Banca Etica established direct links with its stakeholders to enhance the process. They connect their members' interests with the social and economic community needs. That supports how they innovate and create more value that extends beyond them.

Approaches like Banca Etica's provide perspective about what we do from the outside. We receive insights about issues that we might need more awareness of. Creating improvements from external feedback allows us to test our assumptions. The potential to generate more comes from discovering opportunities by changing our thinking. Stepping into spaces to explore and understand interconnectedness leads to new approaches.

Joshua Bates embraces the stakeholder perspective. In his various roles with the Halifax Regional Municipality in Nova Scotia (he is currently Policing Policy Strategist at the Board of Police Commissioners), he has worked with key decision-makers in federal, provincial, and municipal governments. Bates understands how outcomes change when we focus on shared goals. Connection among people, when united by what they care about, encourages innovation. The focus on collective needs shifts thinking in how to meet them in new ways. Bates considers working with stakeholders as a gateway to expanded thinking and outcomes.

Before his current role, one of Bates's favourite projects was at the Halifax Mayor's Office. In 2016, he helped launch a solution for food deserts in remote areas of the municipality. The Mayor voiced that equal access and new opportunities were critical to solving the issue. Bates, working with experts, identified the food-insecure communities far away from grocery stores. He came up with an idea of a mobile food market, following similar approaches implemented by Ottawa and Toronto. City buses could deliver goods to sell in food-insecure communities. Bates worked with stakeholders on how to bring this idea to reality. Conversations held with groups helped flesh out the details to support the local food economy, and they planned the timing of the buses and the types of food to include. Three priorities were identified: affordability, freshness, and cultural appropriateness.

The Mayor's Office worked with grocers to get the lowest price point, and they found retailers with fresh produce.

Instead of bureaucratic approaches, deep insight from those impacted leads to decisions with value. Leaders always have a choice about how to engage stakeholders. We could tick the boxes that show we have connected with stakeholders, but the connections might have been meaningless. The alternative is using authenticity in creating opportunities that lead to material change. Stakeholders bring us into the ecosystem. Learning and developing solutions in that space gets us out of the familiar. Bates, looking ahead, is thinking about how to evolve with the external environment. He's being thoughtful about how to approach his work. He's identifying areas of alignment, and how to pivot his next steps to engage stakeholders. Uncovering perspectives and risks must come with alignment on shared goals. Otherwise, the innovation potential erodes from narrow views of self-serving interests or those that serve one group above others.

What started out as a six-month pilot project is still thriving today. Bates said he and the team at the Mayor's Office couldn't have figured this out on their own. Working closely with stakeholders led to a superior solution with long-term results. Seeing ourselves in the ecosystem offers the path to success. If we remain on the outside, we will struggle to find the way. Our thinking will stay confined to the illusion of separateness.

KEY TAKEAWAYS

- The beliefs of separateness exist all around us. It's an ingrained part of societal norms that we don't question. We fail to understand the implications. We get misled into understanding reality by observing fragmented bits.

- We see only a fraction of what's happening. Seeking the opinions of others provides insight into what we don't notice. We will fail at identifying and connecting pertinent information without feedback from others.

- When teams share a mental model based on a common understanding of shared assumptions, beliefs, and behaviours, collaboration and communication flow easier from clear expectations. When companies have mental models that are not clear, teams work poorly and it's hard to provide guidance. Opaque working environments lead to error-prone execution.

- Shareholder primacy—the belief that shareholder value is the only thing that counts—encourages lines and boundaries between people, entities, and nature. These beliefs produce a transactional and linear approach to running organizations. Looking at value creation only through a financial lens also reduces potential outcomes.

- Awareness of the mental models in an organization is essential to create the future. We need to surface the beliefs that are hidden and can block new ideas. Without knowing the shared beliefs, people use their assumptions. Employees will assume what they think is right, and their choices reflect what makes sense to them. Creating organizational change becomes tough when people use their default beliefs.

- Identifying and setting shared mental models requires ongoing dialogue. Learning to use transparency and explicit assumptions supports conscious choices. We want to find opportunities to reframe people's misaligned assumptions. A place to look for implicit mental models is in our plans for the future. People's thoughts of getting to that point can contain old, new, and unclear assumptions. An organization's core beliefs and the future can remain separate things. Without knowing, the implicit mental models continue.

- Creating visibility of an organization's mental model helps to build shared understanding. The greater insight we can bring into people's perception, the easier it will be for them to spot connections and see patterns. Creating a diagram of the ecosystem enables us to test assumptions. We can identify implicit beliefs, subjective interpretations, and biases. The mind gets familiar with what it sees and loses its ability to spot new patterns and connections. Keeping pace with the external environment requires maintaining awareness. It involves taking what we discover and finding its meaning. Take action based on what is learned and keep repeating the process.

- You can practice interconnectedness in decision-making, engaging with stakeholders, innovation, and discovering opportunities. Establish a decision-making process that helps you think about stakeholders, the impacts on them, and how to maximize value for all. You can also consider how you engage with stakeholders. Do you have one-way connections, or do you ask for their feedback and share information transparently? To discover new opportunities, think as if you are in an ecosystem, and consider the perspective of each stakeholder group. Step outside of your comfort zone and into theirs.

- Getting a sense of your business ecosystem starts with identifying who your stakeholders are and gaining basic insights on what's important to them. But you must go further. Changing the passive connection to an active one creates new sources of innovation. From the outside, you gain perspective about what you do. Let go of those old beliefs of keeping groups away and instead start working with them. Learning about the entire ecosystem gives insight into issues you might lack awareness of. Everything that you uncover provides opportunities. That comes from stepping into spaces to explore interconnectedness by breaking old beliefs. Once you are there, you free yourself from the illusion of separateness.

Step 4: Feel the Future

To be successful in the long run, we must avoid the trap of short-term thinking. Management myopia, the all-too-common dysfunctional behaviour of business leaders, typically leads to trouble. Focusing on short-term profits encourages decisions that favour today over the promise of future value. So leaders fixate on quarterly targets, and end up cutting corners to boost short-term results.

But that only hurts the company later. Just look at the shrinkflation trend. In an attempt to evade consumers' notice, many companies have been reducing the size of their products rather than raise the price. A 2-kilogram bag of sugar shrank to 1.5 kilograms for the same price. Dawn Platinum—a brand of dish soap—went from 479 millilitres to 431 millilitres. Smaller chocolate bars, toilet paper rolls, bags of chips, and the list goes on. But, of course, shoppers did notice. According to an Ipsos poll in the U.S., some 80 percent of consumers said they not only realized they were getting less for the same price but felt cheated. So while the companies that take these actions reap the results on their bottom line in the short term, in the long run they will have tarnished consumer trust—which will affect their future sales.

The business world operates around short-term results. We can thank quarterly reports for that. The pressure to meet targets every three months might invigorate some, but many leaders can't think of the bigger picture under that kind of stress. The "I don't want to deal with it now; we'll worry about it later" blinders offer absolutely no clarity about what exactly will happen later. What will you figure out? Take the annual Conference of the Parties (COP) conference climate pledges. The statements to drastically slash global emissions are well intentioned. But the plans to reach those huge goals? Who knows. It's a sort of self-deception. Leaders tell themselves they're thinking about the future, but they're actually not.

If it's not quarterly reports that have a leader's attention, then it's the three- to five-year business plan, which is also a false presumption of knowing the future. Three to five years is not very long. By the time you get started executing that strategy and working through all the projects you think will deliver, time's up. And what did you achieve? Likely nothing earth-shattering; most likely you've made the familiar slow, steady progress of rolling out new initiatives to change with the times. Management processes to develop these plans are well-intended: Companies truly want to clarify what the future looks like for them so that they can stay competitive and relevant. Everyone is doing their three- to five-year plans—your competitors, and pretty much every company out there. But ambiguity of the future still prevails.

Short-term goals are essential, of course. Strategic plans help individuals and teams focus their efforts on how to proceed into the near-term future. Yet it's just as crucial to think about your organization's long-term future. Yes, you have a vision statement; it's your north star pointing to where you're headed. But you have to articulate that future clearly and create a plan for making your organization's vision a reality. Otherwise, the path forward will remain unclear and unknown.

A few organizations create an eight- or ten-year plan, but leaders have told me that so much can change in the time horizon of a decade that there's no point putting the thought into such plans. I think they're wrong. Take Selfridges, for example. It has succeeded with its long-term future planning. The U.K.-based upscale retailer has put a lot of thought into developing its future aspirations. The 2030 sustainability plan it launched in 2022, called Project Earth, focuses on reinventing retail and creating a sustainable future for its customers. Traditional retailers push the business model of selling more products. But Selfridges has differentiated itself by encouraging consumers to keep products in circulation longer. With its Reselfridges initiative, it will be a marketplace for sustainable clothing as well as a place for consumers to resell, rent, repair, refill, and recycle items. This plan for a total pivot of its retail model has opened up innovation and opportunities. Selfridges found a future that extends beyond its current business model by putting people and the planet at the centre of its long-term transformation.

That kind of thinking means there is a far greater probability that an organization will succeed well into the future. And it's crucial. Over the decades, corporate longevity has been on a downward decline. One study found that, whereas in 1964 the average tenure of S&P 500 companies was 33 years, by 2016 that had contracted to 24 years. It's forecast to contract even further by 2027: to just 12 years. At this rate, about half of the S&P 500 companies over the next 10 years will be replaced. So spending time thinking about the far future is extremely valuable. Without that clarity, and without focus and attention, we don't really know where we're going.

UNCLEAR MEANS IT'S NOT REAL

A future that's not clear is a future that's not real. If it doesn't exist, then we won't perceive what's ahead of us and how best to action the present. Honeywell, for example, missed out on one big trend, the smart-enabled thermostat, when Nest reinvented the thermostat with digital capabilities, unleashing a new era of smart-enabled home devices. But Honeywell won't miss out on future opportunities. The company is now focused on three megatrends: automation, the future of aviation, and energy transition. It has simplified its view of the future to help drive innovation and transformation, and that helps its leadership to allocate capital in the most fruitful ways.

Leaders who don't think through their short-term versus long-term investment plans can easily end up missing opportunities that would have brought great value. Xerox, for example, was convinced its future was to keep selling copying machines—after all, it had dominated the market for so long—not realizing that the technology would die. Blockbuster Video stayed tied to its physical footprint, thinking that consumers would choose going to retail locations over ordering DVDs from the upstart Netflix. Sears, a successful retailer in the 20th century, stuck with its department-store model and catalogue-ordering business, not seeing the market move away from it. These companies couldn't adapt to changing consumer tastes and envision the future.

The cure for short-sightedness is to have a clear, detailed view of the future. We're all capable of it; the answers actually come from within us. (I'll explain how to succeed at developing a clear vision a little later in this chapter.) What we believe the future holds influences our actions in the present. Those beliefs help us make decisions aligned with achieving the future we envision. Our perspectives open up to take risks because we are not trying to grasp for certainty. In other words, we have confidence in the direction we're headed because we have filled the gap between the three- to five-year plan and our vision statement. Achieving profound transformation will come from that foresight.

IT'S HARD TO THINK ABOUT THE FUTURE

So, we know that business leaders need to put more effort into thinking about the future to succeed in this century. But there's one problem. The brain loathes uncertainty, and reacts to it by activating the stress response. That impairs our decision-making and learning functions, making us want to stay close to the familiar and comfortable.

Our brain constantly predicts what's going to happen next *based on what it has become accustomed to*. So predicting the far future for an organization is a real challenge because there isn't a pattern for the brain to leverage in order to project what might happen. There's nothing to assess it against. That's why our plans will bend toward what's similar to the past and present; the element of surprise distresses the brain.

Research shows that when we think about our current self, a region of the brain lights up. But when we consider our future self, a different region activates—the same region as when we think about people we don't know. Our ability to think about the future and visualize different ideas comes from our memories. In fact, Dr. Karl Szpunar, Director of the Memory Lab at Toronto Metropolitan University, found that the brain uses many of the same neural mechanisms to imagine the future as it does to remember the past. Because of that, we can switch from perceiving the present to envisioning alternate realities.

If you or your organization hasn't gone through a particular experience, it's tough to predict that it will happen in the future. This means you will make decisions that may be good for today but could be bad in the long run. So how do you imagine new experiences, new opportunities, for the future? You create the experiences yourself.

When Jeff Bezos first announced Amazon's Prime Air in 2013, a new venture using drones to deliver packages to customers in 30 minutes or less, it was just a vision—a "blue sky" idea that came up when two of Amazon's engineers were chatting over coffee. More than a decade later that concept has come to life, positioned to shape the future of logistics and delivery. Amazon's goal for the end of this decade: To deliver by drone 500 million packages per year, each in less than 60 minutes (and each weighing less than 5 pounds). To get to this point, Amazon began testing its concept, building a strategy, and developing new technology. Early on, it hit a roadblock with U.S. regulations for testing drones. So in 2015 Amazon crossed the border, with permission from the Canadian government, to conduct extensive testing. It took them years to invent, test, and improve the breakthrough technologies. Now they are entering the next phase of Prime Air with a new lighter, quieter drone.

> **PLANNING WITH IMAGINATION**
>
> Let's say you are planning a trip to the Amalfi Coast in Italy. Images come into your mind of a coast lined with villas overlooking the sea. You think of lemon trees and picture yourself eating mini cakes called lemon delight. You envision staying in one of those places perched on the cliff. Maybe you'll hire a boat and explore the nearby sea caves. These images come to mind even though you haven't been to the Amalfi Coast. You've never even seen a lemon tree, stayed at a cliffside villa, or boated into sea caves. That's your brain sourcing information from what you've seen online and in movies, helping you imagine what your future experience might bring.
>
> But as you plan this one, you also recall your past vacations. Perhaps you normally stay in chain hotels near the city centre, and you usually do sightseeing by car or bus. You might decide that's what you really should do for this vacation, too. After all, those habits have never failed you in the past. That's your brain drawing on your past memories to help you

to decide what you'll do in the future. And it can be restricting. The same goes for business planning. When we envision a future scenario, the brain creates a mental scene, like a movie in the mind. There are two memory processes working together to enable this. One helps us forecast possibilities from feelings and visuals. The other checks facts by accessing information that we already know from past experiences—such as timelines and budgets—and that information biases our ideas and shapes what we forecast.

Instead, we need to use information that helps us understand future possibilities—to look for new industries that could emerge, to consider how consumers' needs might shift, and to consider future revolutionary technologies. It's important to play around with ideas of how market dynamics could change. To detach ourselves from the way things are now—and think without boundaries. Preparing information like this ahead of a vision session or future-planning discussion enables people's minds to simulate fresh ideas. As we go through this experience, and do it again, the brain stores the what, where, and when information. That ends up as knowledge for our memory processes to draw upon.

WE NEED FEWER GOALS—AND MORE INTENTION

Many businesspeople fall for the old adage "What gets measured gets done." So they craft numerous goals, and believe they will achieve them all. Organizations end up with a plethora of goals: on strategy, projects, budgets, employee performance plans. Indeed, goals bring discipline and a direction to achieve outcomes. There's no question they are powerful tools. But when you add them up, how many goals do you have—10, 30, 50? And when you put them all together, what does it mean?

It's well known that having too many goals is not good for an organization. It breaks apart people's attention, diluting focus. Also, it's tiresome and draining. We know the brain can't do too many things at once. On top of that, we have to create committees to manage all of the goals and make sure they are met—and sometimes these committees get nothing done, because too many goals represent a lot of different agendas. Making decisions by consensus gets difficult and slows us down.

Yet the idea of reducing the number of goals causes apprehension. Leaders fear that they will choose to focus on the wrong goals. When I chaired a management committee at a financial institution, I was overseeing the execution of strategic initiatives. Every strategic initiative had several goals. The leads of the initiatives often struggled to connect project outcomes with those strategic goals, so their next steps were muddled. The lack of clarity made me wonder why we were even going through the exercise. I brought up my concerns with the company leadership, warning them of the strategic risk of not delivering anything on time, and overstretching resources. The committee decided that all the VPs should get together and cut out some projects so they could focus resources and achieve something of value. But nothing material got cut, and we continued in a marathon that wouldn't end.

Focus is everything in executing a strategy successfully. That means less is more. Leaders must get rid of distractions that hamper people's attention. Steve Jobs and Warren Buffet both learned to say no to most ideas and yes to only the most valuable. In 1997, Jobs cut Apple's product line by 70 percent to focus on just four products. He was well aware of the focus that was necessary to take Apple to the top. As for Buffet, he has veered away from distractions by picking the top five goals for Berkshire Hathaway to focus on, seeing anything beyond five as distractions. And he's right. We only have so much attention and energy, so we must choose well.

SETTING INTENTION

How can we get better at focusing on the right priorities? When we create our short list of goals, we should also set our intentions. Let me explain the difference. Goals are about doing; they are specific and measurable, and represent a future point in time. The rational, analytical nature of goals appeals to the brain, and writing them down supports the brain and body connection. Yet, what gets left out is *how it feels to pursue those goals.* That comes when we state our intentions. Intentions are about being, rather than doing. So when we've crafted our strategic goals, we need to define what we want the experience of achieving them to feel like.

We create intentions all the time, either consciously or subconsciously. When we get dressed or make breakfast, we subconsciously think about what we want to wear or what we want to eat. In our mind, we state it and then take action. For example, we might consciously set an intention to prioritize our well-being. With that comes awareness of how our desired state of well-being will feel, and that provides guidance in crafting our goals and how we achieve them. Let's say one of our well-being goals is to get five days of exercise a week. When we don't end up doing enough, we don't feel as good about ourselves as we'd imagined; we haven't met our original intention to prioritize our wellness.

Intentions complete the experience of goal-setting by connecting feelings and intuition with actions. Consciously stating intentions helps us see the bigger picture, shifting the focus to what we will experience through our actions. We notice the experience in the present while we work toward the goal.

A study by the Max Planck Institute for Human Cognitive and Brain Sciences discovered how the brain stores intentions. Experiments revealed that intentions do not encode in single neurons but cover the whole spatial pattern of brain activity. The front brain regions store the intention and, when it's time to execute it, the intention copies to a different area of the brain.

Dr. Bruce Lipton, stem cell biologist and author of *The Biology of Belief*, researched how cells receive and process information. The brain communicates information to all the cells in the body, and they respond accordingly. He found that when we set an intention our cells will act in alignment with it, vibrating at a consistent frequency. Conversely, our cells respond to negative thoughts by preparing the nervous system's fight-or-flight response.

Leaders need both goals and intentions because employees need to feel a connection with the future that leaders want to create. Goals support motivation and will, enabling the brain's ability to plan and focus attention. Intentions can help galvanize a collective experience for the organization because we're declaring what we intend to accomplish through our actions. This commitment to the journey keeps us honest in focusing on only a few goals—five maximum, but ideally just one.

Sometimes intention statements show up as a commitment, or as an aspiration. Take Mejuri, a Toronto-based jeweller. Its mission statement is "Rethink the way we purchase jewellery—for ourselves." But it goes further by stating its intention: "Turn fine jewelry into an everyday occasion while working toward making a positive impact in our communities, the industry, and the world." That statement informs Mejuri's focus on sustainability, responsible design and sourcing, and commitment to people. It guides the company's decision-making.

You can set intentions for your organization's future and key strategic initiatives. Remember that when we are intentional about the future, our focus is on what we are doing now, and why. Articulating our future intention goes beyond the mechanics of goals, and engages emotions and intuition to help us understand how to actually make our goals a reality.

HOW TO SET PERSONAL INTENTIONS

Setting intentions for ourselves is a powerful way to orient the mind. It can be done at the start of a day, week, or month to help guide the mind to achieve outcomes. Intentions can be applied to whatever we want to experience in life, whether it's being more successful at work, improving our health, or facing life's challenges in a positive way.

I like to set intentions at the beginning of every day, week, and month. Yes, it sounds like a lot. But it's just a simple statement, and I find it keeps my focus on what's important in a given time frame. On Sunday mornings, for example, I will say to myself, "My intention is to enjoy the day." For years, I used to get Sunday morning dread. I'd look ahead at the week, start feeling anxious—and then start working. But since I started setting my intention, and sticking to it, my attitude and behaviour shifted. No more Sunday dread.

You don't have to write your intentions down. You can say them out loud or in your head. What's key is that you feel what you're saying: your feelings must match your thoughts. Here are some example statements.

"I intend to…"

- Focus my attention on the experience instead of the to-do list.
- Slow down and be fully present with my family.
- Put myself first rather than pleasing others.
- Listen to my intuition as my guidance.
- Surround myself with relationships that are uplifting.
- Use my talents and gifts to accelerate my career.

Practising setting intentions for yourself will give you experience as well as insights into how to leverage them to achieve results. That will help you to develop intentions in the workplace.

ENVISION THE FUTURE

When we are faced with making a choice that will significantly impact our personal future, a simple list of pros and cons can help us make a decision. But as the neuroscience proves, really thinking about and actually imagining what-ifs can put us in a better position to succeed. This is not mind-wandering, since it's deliberate. When I had to decide whether to move from Vancouver to Toronto, I wrote down the pros and cons of each option. But then I took it a step further and envisioned what my life might feel like in the future if I stayed in B.C. versus what it might feel like if I moved to Ontario. In my imagination I came up with various simulations of the future, which uncovered deeper insights and drew out what was most important to me for my future. Really imagining it provided an experience, one in which I felt the right choice in my gut. And here I am in Toronto.

Simulating possibilities for life choices helps us make decisions for the future. We need to do the same in business. In 2023, NASA completed a successful mission of a crew simulating living and working on Mars for 378 days. It had created a 1,700-square-foot, 3D-printed habitat to mimic the Red Planet. The crew conducted "Marswalks" and robotic operations, did habitat maintenance, exercised, and grew crops. They also faced some challenging scenarios to give insights into how to deal with them if humans ever do spend time on Mars: environmental stressors were introduced such as resource limitations, isolation, and confinement. This mission has provided NASA with critical data to validate systems and develop technological solutions for future missions. Simulating the future will help NASA reach its goal of sending astronauts to Mars as soon as the 2030s.

NASA's approach helps human beings to feel the future by experiencing it. Simply brainstorming ideas or discussing concepts for the future isn't enough. If we are going to understand the future of our organization, we need to design it in a way that transports our senses so that we can see and feel it. We need to develop a long-term commitment for what we want to achieve. Thus, feeling a connection to the future is a must. It will help us see risks differently, so that rather than fearing them, we allow opportunities to emerge.

The key to imagining the future for an organization is to simulate it through experiences. To envision future possibilities, people must work with what already lives in their memory to see themselves in the future story. That opens up their ability to work with details to build solutions and ideas. They can get past fear-limiting thoughts, and instead play with possibilities.

That future story requires details. The NASA astronauts on the Mars mission likely recorded how they felt about experiences, ideas, and possible risks. Leveraging methods like prototyping, role-playing, and digital technology results in active experiences. You want to create an environment where people interact and design the future.

When I helped develop the vision and strategy for Vancity Community Investment Bank, my team and I organized several envisioning sessions with various participants—the board of directors, senior leaders, and a diverse group of employees from across the organization. Each session had a different focus to gain perspectives on future possibilities. For example, one focused on key trends in Canada by 2040. We put ourselves into that future, and brainstormed, and eventually we came up with a vision for what forces we thought would shape the needs of Canadians in the future—forces such as wealth divergence and increased income inequality, climate change, food insecurity, and affordable housing. We showcased the areas of opportunity to potentially focus the bank's long-term vision for how best to channel capital. After the sessions, the bank's future emerged: it became the first social finance bank in Canada.

> **MANAGING SUCCESSFUL ENVISIONING SESSIONS**
>
> To manage successful sessions, planning is essential to develop a well-defined agenda with facilitation. A facilitator can keep participants on track and focused. Including participants that represent stakeholders will give greater perspectives that represent the ecosystem. Before holding a session, give participants time to review materials relevant to the future. Avoid giving them constraints.
>
> Envisioning the future requires being present, so have people put their devices away. Try to think at least 10 years ahead. The facilitator can prompt the group with questions about how they imagine the future, such as:
>
> - What is happening in the world with people and with the climate?
> - What is the state of globalization and cooperation?
> - What's happening in the country and the places where you do business?
> - What is happening in the lives of your customers, suppliers, partners, and industry bodies?
> - What do people need?
> - What new industries, innovations, and technologies have emerged?
> - How has your industry evolved?

As you go through each question, allow time for people to write down their thoughts and feelings—whatever comes to them. Then, after each question, engage in dialogue to share what people discovered. Do not assess or analyze what is being said. Also, this isn't a brainstorming exercise so do not generate a list of ideas. Once you complete the dialogue, pause for few moments. Reflect together to understand what has been unearthed. Then ask:

- What is your organization doing in this imagined future?
- How is it responding to the needs of people, and the planet?
- What influence and role is your organization playing in the future?
- Is the organization in a new space, the same space, or additional space?
- What does it feel like inside your organization?
- How do your customers and other stakeholders feel about it?
- What kind of relationships or partnerships does your organization have in this imagined future?

It's likely that you will need more than one envisioning session to get a full picture, but each experience people undergo creates learning and will add to how they perceive the future.

Engaging the brain in a visual experience and thinking about success helps reduce stress about what might come and creates motivation. In turn, that success is much more likely.

> After you've envisioned the future, define your organization's future intention. For example, a health insurance company could set the intention "Our services meet customers' needs through every life stage to empower choices for a lifetime of wellness." Or, "We keep people's well-being at the centre of everything we do." These intentions could lead the company down two different paths. The first focuses on product and service innovation. The latter creates a business model and operational innovation for a customer-centric approach. Either option can lead to success. Intentions have the power to bring conviction about the path you choose. With the intention in place, you're set to craft a few strategic goals. Then you can take ideas into concepts for development and testing.

Intention brings the future into today's daily experiences and guides what we're becoming: we feel it, be it, and act it. Our actions flow in greater alignment, which also shifts behaviour. This awareness expands our perception and focuses attention like a bridge to the future. We can more easily brush distractions aside and focus on what's most important: actually achieving our organization's future.

> **YOUR FUTURE SELF**
>
> Imagining the future and setting the intention will help your organization, but be sure to think about your own future with respect to your leadership. Knowing where you are going gives you the inspiration and confidence to make choices now that are right for you for the long term.

Your future self is part of you. When you become present and quiet the mind, you can hear the guidance that connects with your goals and aspirations. Yet society, education, and work environments have taught us to look at ourselves from the perspective of the past, not of who we will become. Take the resumé: On it, you present yourself from the past to get a future opportunity. Yes, there's value in showing your background and expertise. But who will you be in the future? Is that not a relevant factor in determining your potential for career success?

So how do you discover your future self? In quiet moments alone, get out of mental chatter. Ask yourself a few questions and note your answers. Writing things down as opposed to putting them in your smartphone helps to uncover connections, and you might see a pattern. Bring your attention to what you sense in your heart, body, and intuition when you ask yourself the following questions

- What has my gut been trying to tell me? What have I ignored and not given attention to?

- What have I noticed about myself? What thoughts have crossed my mind about my life ahead that I have not given attention to?

- What will I be doing in the future? What's happening around me now and how do I feel?

- What areas of my life do I need to align to serve my path better?

- What do I need to do now that will help create change and new experiences for myself?

> You may be comfortable with the present, and know exactly who you are. Yet sticking with the status quo hinders your personal development, and the potential of your organization. Gaining clarity about your future self helps to carve out a better path for learning. And the more you envision it, the less hesitation and doubt you will have about not only your own future but that of your organization.

KEY TAKEAWAYS

- Business environments encourage short-term thinking that keeps the status quo. Short-sightedness leaves out significant perspectives of the future. It doesn't take into account the business's ecosystem, which is constantly changing. This constrains a business's ability to innovate, solve problems, and handle day-to-day issues. The impact is not knowing where decisions and actions lead. A future that's not clear is a future that's not real. Misinformed observations and erroneous conclusions will take us off course.

- If we can create a clear and convincing vision of the future, it will affect how we act today. The lens of the future can be a source of innovation. It also provides the means to question assumptions and challenge beliefs. The way we describe the future contains the ideas that influence actions. The greater our vantage point, the more intelligence we have to guide our actions.

- We struggle to think about the future because the brain loathes uncertainty. If we can't reduce uncertainty, then the stress response activates and we stay close to the familiar and comfortable. Our brain always predicts what's going to happen next. But predicting the future is hard since there's nothing to assess it against. That's why our future plans will look similar to the past and present.

- How we think about the future is based on our memories. If we haven't lived through something, we can't imagine it happening in the future. This biases our decision-making, and we will choose decisions that are good for today despite being worse in the long run. To imagine new possibilities, we need to create new experiences.

- Too many goals lead to poor execution, so it's important to create fewer goals and to set intentions. Goals are specific and measurable—they are about doing, and focus on what and when. Intentions are about being—they bring focus to what we will experience through our actions and help us see the bigger picture. We need both.

- Intentions can create a collective experience for our organization. Employees need to feel a connection with the future. When we set an intention, we imagine it, and think and act like we've already experienced it. We state what we intend to accomplish through our actions, and this commitment to the journey keeps us focused. We can set intentions for our organization's future or for key strategic initiatives.

- Simulating a possible future enables a deeper understanding of it. We need to create and design the future, immersing in the experience of it. The key to envisioning the future is to create new experiences for our employees. People need to see themselves in the future that we as leaders aspire to create. These experiences open up their ability to take ideas into concepts for development and testing.

- The more we simulate the future, the more we enable people's perception. Leveraging methods like prototyping, role-playing, and digital technology creates active experiences. Make the environment one where people can interact, collaborate, and design. After envisioning the future, set your future intention and define key goals. You will have the clarity of what you're becoming, and that makes execution much easier.

Step 5: Think with Abundance

Too often, we see the glass as half empty. When we don't get that job we wanted, we can feel low about it. In that moment, we don't think about other, better opportunities that will come up. Think of those weight-loss programs that restrict calories. It's the thoughts of "can't have" that dominate the mind, and food is no longer enjoyable. And consider those emails from retailers that flood our inboxes every year: "Black Friday Sale! Buy now before it's too late!" We become anxious that we'll miss out on something good, and we get a feeling of urgency in the pit of our stomachs. The so-called FOMO (fear of missing out) actually prompts buying behaviour because we think we'll lose if we don't take action.

This is the scarcity mindset at work. Our attention shifts to the scarce item rather than to what we have. The resource could be time, money, or social connection—whatever we think we need—and the perception of it matters more than an actual lack of resources does. Often, people don't realize this because their thoughts fixate, and they can't see it any other way.

Words like *can't, need, want,* and *don't have* signify scarcity beliefs. Repeating these words every day forms habitual thought patterns, so we don't notice how often we use that language. And it's hard to escape the scarcity mindset since it's everywhere: It prevails in media, business, economics, politics, and people we interact with. In our personal lives, we might unknowingly compare ourselves to others, and think about what we don't have. In organizations, scarcity thinking hinders risk-taking, innovation, teamwork, and planning for the future. It's not necessarily doom-and-gloom thinking, but the subtlety of "not enough" makes people believe organizational goals are hard to reach.

In the workplace, the scarcity mindset finds its way into decisions and activities in the normal course of business. For instance, leaders will discuss insufficient capital, budget, time, or talent. It becomes a routine conversation to move resources around to make ends meet, framing resources as finite. This short-term mindset limits what we can achieve and hijacks thoughts to focus on what we have to lose. Forget long-term planning; we don't have the mental capacity for it. Leaders will find themselves on a slower, predictable path for growth. Meanwhile, the opportunity cost balloons from missed prospects and a risk aversion to testing new ideas.

The challenge with the scarcity mindset is that if we don't notice it, we don't know what it's doing to us. Seeing the glass as half empty becomes a part of how we perceive experiences. But thinking that way affects how we feel. The scarcity mindset induces stress and can take a toll on mental health. Negative emotions lead to using coping mechanisms that are about now, such as cutting corners. That might save time but will make things worse in the long run. Leaders often fall into this trap when making decisions about strategy, investments, and pursuing opportunities: those decisions gravitate toward hitting short-term targets.

Culture suffers, too, in organizations with the scarcity mindset. Research shows that scarcity encourages competitive behaviour rather than the camaraderie of working toward a common goal. The mentality is "I win, you lose," an unhealthy form of competition that comes from a fear-based view of a shrinking pie. Leaders hoard talent and resources for their agenda. If things go well, these individuals take credit. But if things go wrong, they blame others or do not acknowledge it.

In *Scarcity: Why Having Too Little Means So Much*, Princeton University professor Eldar Shafir and Harvard University economist Sendhil Mullainathan study people's minds and identify inefficiencies. Shafir states that scarcity takes up "mental bandwidth" that would otherwise go to planning, problem-solving, and less urgent matters. These preoccupations cause a mental deficit, making us prone to mistakes and ineffective decision-making. Furthermore, we block access to our intuition. Our inner state can be set off balance because feelings of lack are powerful and distracting the mind. We reduce our ability to be present and understand what's happening in the moment.

Other symptoms of a scarcity mindset include over-scheduling and saying yes to things when we should say no. We end up stretched. Leaders find themselves in a self-inflicted battle where they will remain stuck unless they break the cycle. The scarcity mindset will not act as a source of innovation. Fighting over the same pie with finite pieces will never be enough. So the challenge for us as leaders is to transform a scarcity mindset to one of abundance.

New solutions and opportunities do exist—as long as we choose to believe they do. When we think with an abundance mindset, we perceive limitless potential. When we're faced with challenges, our outlook does not have to get bogged down by limiting thoughts. The abundance mindset helps us think through the lens of plenty, even when faced with adversity. Nelson Mandela, the first democratically elected black president of South Africa, didn't stop his mission for a free, just, and equitable country while living out a prison life sentence. He led with hope, not resorting to violence, and showed dignity and forgiveness as a means to lead South Africa forward after his release. Mandela remained committed to a long-term vision, enduring a tumultuous journey that inspired human rights globally.

An abundance mindset helps us get through challenges because it encourages us to perceive limitless potential. We go through experiences knowing that many chances, choices, and opportunities exist. We have an appreciation for what we have. So, that helps us focus on outcomes even if our resources are low. In that regard, thoughts of abundance help us make decisions that are better for the future. The mind stays open to thinking through broader perspectives and possibilities. Ridding ourselves of scarcity frees our cognitive capacity for new thinking and solving problems. We have better control of our attention and the effectiveness of working memory. An abundance mindset helps us spot connections and consider the unknown, focusing our thinking on "how to" rather than "cannot." The shift gives us a way to rethink how best to achieve goals. When we focus our attention on the experience, we will be more receptive to change.

When it comes to business, thinking with abundance can help us avoid fear-based thinking and gives others the mental bandwidth to look ahead. Along with that, supporting an attitude of openness nurtures a cultural environment that embraces change. Employees are more willing to accept situations and less likely to criticize others. The focus is on expanding and getting the most out of each experience. And all of this leads to resilience and an ability to flow with moment-to-moment experiences. You'll feel inclined to learn and to find new insights that evolve thinking, whether for you or for the collective organization.

Leading with a willingness to learn helps orient people to possibilities and growth. They, too, start shifting their mindset to notice that the world is full of opportunities. The change in attitude among employees enables a faster path to transformation. There's more positive energy in the organization. Eileen Fisher, a socially conscious American fashion designer and retailer, integrated sustainability in her business strategy long before it became a trend. The company has a mantra of "business as a movement" to inspire daily actions that support the continued success of the business, while acting as an agent of change. It believes it has an impact in all the ways it touches people. When it comes to big decisions, they often emerge from employees' passion about a concept. That sparks a bunch of smaller decisions, which build into something bigger. And that's abundance in action: when you empower employees and encourage small actions, they accumulate into a larger, positive impact.

That's why Eileen Fisher advocates for employees to know that all the little choices matter—they all add up and collectively create social impact. Every action has the possibility to create value and positive connections. Salespeople at Eileen Fisher stores have been trained to help customers choose the garment that will make them feel more confident. Employees working with fabrics source sustainable materials and question whether a fabric works for the company and its suppliers. Stores have the autonomy to plan events based on what they feel matters to their customers. Some stores act as gathering spaces for events like book swaps. One location is experimenting with new ideas, such as hosting craft workshops using scrap fabrics; it has harnessed a renewed community interest in crafts by becoming a part of it.

When a company has a culture of collaboration, leadership maintains openness with employees and encourages them to grow in ways that work for who they are. In this scenario, leadership doesn't act like it has all the right answers. Rather, it seeks the perspectives of many before deciding to move forward in a particular direction. Learning, which is at the core of this approach, helps the company discover a fresh way of doing things. And that's what's happening at Eileen Fisher to enable continuous innovation, with respect to its aspiration of being 100 percent sustainable. A company that thinks with abundance is better able to make goal-oriented decisions. Leaders will have greater confidence in these choices and in taking risks.

FASHION TACKLES SCARCITY

The fashion industry notoriously pollutes the planet and wastes natural resources. Fashion brands have stuck with the business model of "produce more," so consumers buy more. It's a volume business, and that's not good for the planet. To make a single pair of jeans, it takes a staggering 1,800 gallons of water. Meanwhile, two billion people worldwide don't have access to safe drinking water, and nearly half of the global population faces severe water scarcity for at least a part of the year. Levi Strauss & Co. decided to embrace water scarcity head on by rethinking its business model and production processes. The company decided it must *sell less* and tackle consumer overconsumption.

The change in direction has compelled company innovation. Levi's keeps tabs on factories where local suppliers are up against greater water stress. These facilities must innovate to reuse water or create new low-water finishes. Jennifer DuBuisson, Levi Strauss's senior director of sustainability, says, "Whenever an idea is radical, it takes time to change the mindset. But once facilities realized these techniques weren't only saving water, they're saving money, people quickly came on board." Levi's response to a global problem demonstrates thinking with abundance. The 18th-century denim-maker doesn't plan to reduce its revenue but rather to find new ways to create value. Their goal is to sell fewer new products, and instead grow other sources of revenue such as a repair and resell shop. They're also improving manufacturing practices to better adapt to demand and to avoid excess inventory. Water is a scarce resource. Yet that reality isn't

> limiting the company's ability to make a cool pair of jeans that lasts, and that consumers love, like the 501 jean introduced in the late 1800s.

IT'S ALL ABOUT GRATITUDE

How can you develop an abundance mindset? It requires new thought patterns, habits, and behaviours, and shifting focus to appreciate what you have through gratitude. Getting familiar with your mindset requires being present and noticing your thoughts. For example, if you notice thoughts about a solution not working, consider why you think that. Did something similar happen in the past? If so, then recognize the assumptions that bias your thoughts. If not, consider if you're judging circumstances too quickly and not thinking critically. Simple attention to your thoughts can unravel the old patterns and underlying beliefs. Every chance you get to evaluate your thoughts, try to find what's hidden. Replacing those views lets you create new neural pathways. Allowing beliefs to surface and discussing them with others boosts learning for everyone. Your colleagues and teams pick up on it and begin spotting ideas that don't work and reframing them with a lens of abundance.

Self-reflection and awareness play a crucial part in reprogramming your thought patterns. You can also help strengthen neural connections to think with abundance through gratitude. Gratitude is a state of mind, a feeling in the heart of appreciation or thankfulness. You can practice gratitude by expressing it to yourself and others. The repetitive practice helps increase neuron density and leads to higher emotional intelligence. Studies show that over time, it improves physical and mental health. It also increases happiness and promotes better sleep.

Researchers looked at which areas of the brain activate with gratitude. The regions that show increased activity include those associated with empathy, reward, moral and social cognition, and value judgment. Gratitude also activates the hypothalamus. This region produces effects on stress, metabolism, and regulating hormones for vital functions such as body temperature, emotional responses, appetite, and sleep. The hypothalamus releases the neurochemical dopamine, the feel-good hormone. So, the brain learns to notice and find things to be grateful for. And because it feels good, that supports creating new habits.

The essential aspect of building a gratitude practice is experiencing it daily. Effective gratitude practices activate certain circuits of the heart. Those effects help us establish a sustainable way of being. But we need to go beyond creating a simple list of what we're grateful for and develop a practice that resonates with us. One of the most potent forms of gratitude is receiving thanks. When we give genuine thanks to others, we have a profound effect on their neurology and help shift their mindset. Research on gratitude shows that employees who feel valued have higher job satisfaction. They also engage in productive relationships and feel motivated to achieve shared goals. Practising the abundance mindset does far more than produce benefits for ourselves; abundance extends to those around you and offers the chance to create a greater good that benefits everyone.

Shifting to an abundance mindset does not happen overnight. It takes continuous effort, and requires patience and observation. If thoughts of scarcity cross your mind, bring awareness to them and notice what triggered them. At first, the reasons for scarcity thinking might be unclear. But after a while, you will start to see your habitual nature. You can decide how to reframe those beliefs, and you will want to. The abundance mindset can alter the brain's circuitry to perceive with a different outlook. We can learn to think with gratitude, empathy, contentment, and reciprocity. But it takes practice to sustain a default mindset of abundance.

Language and the way we use our words is powerful. Thoughts, whether spoken or unspoken, carry meaning, feelings, and intentions. Paying attention to the inner dialogue of what you think about yourself is vital—you want to catch the thought patterns that do not serve you. Sometimes, how you describe yourself or what you're doing contains limiting thoughts that you don't notice. The repetition of these ideas is a cause for concern. You may start to believe what you think and reinforce those beliefs. The influence can lead to behaviours and actions that put you in a cycle you don't notice. For example, I've heard authors say they aren't looking to win a literary award when they release their book. I observe that as defensive behaviour with underlying thoughts of self-doubt. Maybe they feel it's best to hedge when in public, but that is scarcity thinking.

Finding these limiting thoughts tucked far away in your mind matters a lot. Dissipating the beliefs that hinder your growth will help you build an abundance mindset. Observing how you view the world, opportunities, and the future identifies whether scarcity lurks in your beliefs. These are obstacles within you. You have the power to change them through your attention. You can release the ideas that hold you back and encourage scarcity thinking. Once you do, you need to replace them with new thinking patterns.

Gratitude practices can help create new mental pathways that build the abundance mindset. Learning to appreciate what we have helps alleviate the thoughts of not enough. The brain needs to feel that we are okay. When we don't feel that way, anxiety, stress, and fight-or-flight are the body's responses. We mustn't compare ourselves to others. Comparisons with others' successes or misfortunes direct energy away from us. Fuelling envy or a false sense of gratefulness does not produce anything beneficial. Instead, focus on appreciating life's journey.

> **HOW TO PRACTISE GRATITUDE**
>
> Gratitude is appreciation and acceptance of the present. Paying attention to yourself is the part of self-care that allows you to receive more abundance. Experiencing abundance feels difficult when we hold on to mistakes and lack self-forgiveness, and the resulting negative emotions cloud the way we perceive. Developing your new gratitude practices will take trial and error, so do what works for you and pay attention to *how you feel*. Here are a few suggestions for how to create the intent to think with abundance and immerse yourself in the experience.
> - Write down a few things you are grateful for in a journal. It is best to find a time in the day when you can have a few moments of quiet reflection. Don't treat this as a list-making activity. Feel connected

with what you write and the story behind it. You can do this daily, or write it down once and remind yourself every day.

- Speak positive affirmations out loud to yourself. These are "I am" statements that fit what you need to hear at this point in your life. For example, "I am content," "I am healthy," "I am thriving," "I am abundant," "I am strong," "I am blessed," and "I am successful." These statements help your mind believe it's happening now along with the associated feelings.

- Create a daily mindfulness meditation practice, whether for a few minutes or more. A free meditation app, such as Insight Timer, can help you start and build habits for a new practice. If you feel unsure about meditation, begin with instrumental meditation music. Listen to it with a clear mind, and use it to pause and reset.

- Use breathwork, cold baths, and activities that engage the nervous system. These practices can help shift neural circuitry toward pro-social thinking and behaviours. Resetting the nervous system helps you to perceive and gain clarity. It opens your ability to think with abundance and feel gratitude.

- Take small actions daily to achieve something you want. It could be anything—a hobby, wellness goal, or new habit you want to embed in your life. After all the small steps, the achievement helps your mind think with abundance. You can see progress, and that feels good.

> Developing your practices can take time. Allow yourself to be in the experience. As science shows, it can change the brain structure and neural processing, so it's well worth the effort. After all, you are investing in yourself.

LEADING WITH THE ABUNDANCE MINDSET

Nurturing the abundance mindset in the workplace takes ongoing awareness and deliberate actions. Replacing thoughts of scarcity begins with beliefs and understanding the implications. If you follow your thoughts and see where they lead, be open to what you observe. Encouraging other leaders and employees to do the same will surface patterns and themes. You will discover scarcity embedded in how you work and what you produce. You will notice it in decision-making processes and how you manage the performance of people and the organization. The best way to evolve from entrenched scarcity is by shifting the collective organizational mindset to abundance.

Influencing people to think about possibilities and new approaches takes consistent effort. It's easier not to change—spiralling down a path of pessimism comes without trying. Defensive circuits in the brain are strong because they help keep us safe, and that makes automatic and habitual thinking hard for people to resist when they lack awareness of their thought processes. Thus, we must be ready to work alongside others to support new thinking and behaviour.

Mindset influences our attitude and actions; core beliefs and assumptions allow us to orient ourselves to a set of expectations, explanations, and goals. Mindset determines how we interpret situations and respond to them. We tend to use them habitually, and don't notice when we do. We can reprogram beliefs, but if we are going to intentionally shift our thinking we have to be aware of them in the first place. When we cross over from the scarcity mindset to abundance, we see different opportunities and ways we can innovate and transform.

So how do you pivot to spotting scarcity in your organization and reframing it? First off, don't overwhelm yourself by trying to uncover it in each conversation because this kind of thinking lurks everywhere. Instead, be aware of how you coach and guide teams. Find meaningful opportunities to shift the team's thinking. When you discuss risks, potential, and new opportunities with your colleagues, pay attention to scarcity thinking.

Employees often think with scarcity when they tell you that they need more resources. This a common request that you likely hear all the time. Employees perceive there's too much work and not enough people to do it. It's much easier to point to a lack of resources than re-examine ideas and how the work is approached. When you notice people getting caught in this thought process, help them step back.

I have encountered many of these situations. Every time I got a request for more resources, I questioned why, to try to understand what was really going on. It would always come down to three things that needed clarity: outcomes, expectations, and steps on the path. I observed employees spinning in circles, dwelling in self-doubt, and getting frustrated. They would compromise their mental capacity with the stress they brought upon themselves. So of course that leads to working slowly and inefficiently, making mistakes, and missing deadlines.

I tackled this by asking people to let go of the thought of more resources and just think about how to achieve the desired outcome. Did they consider alternatives? What assumptions were they making? I would hear, "We don't want to re-invent the wheel." And my response to that was, "There is no wheel. Find a new way." Their minds were then freed from their attachment to scarcity, which led to getting creative in reaching outcomes better and faster. That approach has consistently helped me throughout my career to reduce headcount and find efficiencies instead of maintaining big, unproductive teams.

REGENERATION MATTERS

Innovation and transformation are key to spotting and reframing scarcity thinking in an organization and replacing it. Approaching that with abundance leads to new forms of value. The scarcity mindset is closed and linear, and entrenched in transactional business models: sell goods or services for monetary value. Businesses in the 21st century need the opposite model if we are going to succeed in a new future. They need a regenerative model. Nature uses that kind of continuous cycle to seed resiliency in ecosystems to endure disruptions, damage, and healing through creation, growth, and restoration.

Regenerative business practices have emerged in the agriculture, retail, food/beverage, and fashion sectors, with new methods focused on renewing energy and materials in sustainable systems that extend life. Developing new systems and practices provides opportunities to innovate and transform like never before. Profound change starts with changing our mindset to see circular connections and patterns. It sounds simple yet it's a significant shift from the kind of linear thinking that's driven by scarcity.

> **HOW CHOCOLATE CAN CHANGE THE WORLD**
>
> Alter Eco, a France-based organic snack food company, uses regenerative agriculture practices to grow cacao. Industrial farming practices deplete the soil and create vulnerability to drought and pests. But this company has developed a farming model to produce cacao beans grown in dynamic agroforestry, which means it replicates an abundant forest ecosystem by planting banana, shade, cacao, and timber trees. Many benefits result from soil fertility and biodiversity; the natural environment becomes drought-resistant and provides farmers with a better working environment and more shade. Alter Eco actively supports farmers in the chocolate supply chain to transition to regenerative agriculture. Currently, it has 400 cacao farmers in Ecuador using these practices, and it aspires to make the regenerative farming model available to the entire cacao industry. Alter Eco estimates that the environmental impact of doing so would be equivalent to taking 27 million cars off the road for 20 years.

Redesigning end-to-end solutions with new utility and business models can create new market spaces. Pivoting from transactional and linear approaches opens reciprocity and relationships. With that change, we create the potential to bring more value for stakeholders because the lens of abundance allows us to rethink what we do and how to regenerate value. Jeff Bos, founder of Foment Regeneration, a consultancy, enables leaders and companies to build a regenerative future. Foment works with companies across many sectors to deliver experiences that act as a catalyst for change. They facilitate experiences to open up new thinking in workshops, retreats, and communities of practice. These experiences inspire a cultural transformation that starts from within. Bos describes regenerative thinking as "orienting to the continual unfolding of systems." When you bring openness to what you think about the external environment, your perception shifts. You notice the external environment in motion to inspire how you design solutions.

As a part-time executive, Bos supports the work of the Soil & Climate Initiative. Green America, a non-profit environmental organization, launched the program. The initiative intends to increase the number of acres in regenerative agriculture. Building soil health is paramount to support humanity sustainably into the future. Almost all the food we consume—95 percent of it—relies on soil. Yet the 2050 outlook, according to the UN's Food and Agriculture Organization, estimates that 90 percent of all soil will degrade. The consequences of that put natural ecosystems, climate, and food security at risk for all.

The Soil & Climate Initiative has built a network to share insights with stakeholders. Those lessons help farmers, supply chains, and other entities evolve using regenerative practices. Making the transition from chemical-based farming to biological farming represents a massive shift. Beliefs, behaviours, and actions change from mechanistic to understanding living systems. The farmers shift deep beliefs from "I know how to farm" to "I don't know how to farm."

Bos shared a story about one of the Nebraska farmers he's working with. The farmer told him that he used to wake up thinking about what he was going to kill—namely, weeds and pests with pesticides, herbicides, and fungicides, which also kill much other biology in the soil. Now that farmer wakes up thinking about how he can bring more life into the farm that day. He was able to switch his way of thinking because he reconnected with the soil to understand it through a different lens. Also, working in the network with other farmers provided a critical connection and support mechanism. Bos says that once you have a profound shift in mindset that changes your consciousness, you can't go back. You can't forget what you have discovered.

The more we grasp the external environment in constant motion, the better we can pivot linear thinking to finding new ways to create transformation.

As you may recall from Step 4: Feel the Future, the U.K.-based retailer Selfridges pivoted its business model to encourage consumers to keep products in circulation longer. They added new streams of revenue from reuse, repair, and reselling services. Their transformation is about circular practices: they create regeneration by getting more out of products and their lifecycles. The retailer pays attention to production and consumption to create more and reduce environmental harm. But to design out waste and pollution, it takes collaboration with ecosystem stakeholders. Redesigning end-to-end solutions in this way opens a path to new market spaces.

Thousand Fell, an NYC-based footwear brand, believes material innovation is its superpower. So, it wants to use that to create high-quality products that serve people and the planet. How? It redesigned its products' life cycle with circular, regenerative thinking by creating the world's first recyclable sneaker and reminding people that "sneakers are not trash." A whopping 97 percent of shoes go to landfills because the materials are not recyclable. Pioneering a recyclable sneaker meant rethinking material sourcing and production. Thousand Fell designed out waste and pollution in its manufacturing by applying circular principles: It figured out how to recycle 70 percent of the weight of a shoe into a new product. The rest gets upcycled to a new use, downcycled to reuse material, or composted.

Thousand Fell innovated the classic white sneaker with natural, regenerative materials so that the shoes stay in use longer thanks to durability, repelling water, and resisting stains. The sneakers have an aloe vera insole liner and a protective quartz finish to keep them white. So it's giving customers what they seek—stylish shoes—but also educates them on circularity in the fashion industry. When customers finish with their sneakers, Thousand Fell pays for the shipping and recycling, and sends them a $20 credit toward the next pair. (Wearable sneakers go to Soles4Souls, a non-profit organization that helps those in need.) Thousand Fell's innovation showcases how value creation remains trapped in linear practices, and that product superiority and captivating consumers can go hand in hand with caring for the planet.

Embarking on a new path with new thinking is a significant experience. When we stop changing how we think, the world around us ceases to evolve. We must learn to trust ourselves and the emerging direction that looks different from today and the past. Practising the abundance mindset will lead us into the future. Unlike the scarcity mindset, it will not take us back to a place where there is less choice and less opportunity. All that stands in our way is how we think—and we can change that.

> **KEY TAKEAWAYS**
>
> - The scarcity mindset comes from a perspective of lacking. It also gets influenced by feelings of competition. When we experience scarcity, our attention shifts to the scarce item. The resource could be time, money, social connection, or something else we need. Thoughts of scarcity are rooted in psychology; the perception of it matters more than an actual lack of resources.
>
> - When we believe we don't have enough, it takes hold of our attention. It influences our thinking, behaviour, and decision-making. In organizations, the scarcity mindset hinders risk-taking, innovation, teamwork, and thinking about the future. The problem with the scarcity mindset is that we don't realize the effects of it, since the beliefs become a part of how we perceive experiences. The mindset also induces stress and negative emotions. That leads to behaviours focused only on the now. We could make decisions that make us worse off in the long run.
>
> - Scarcity thinking dampens decision-making. Considering resources as finite, such as capital, budget, time, or

talent, limits what we can achieve. Behaviours such as resisting change and avoiding risks influence short-term thinking. The brain gets stressed out, and it becomes hard to think. Working memory declines and people struggle to retain information in the immediate moment. Leaders with a scarcity mindset will find themselves on a slower, predictable, linear path for growth.

- Having an abundance mindset means thinking through the lens of plenty. We perceive limitless potential. We understand that many chances, choices, and opportunities exist. We can focus on outcomes even if our resources are low. Thinking with abundance allows us to make better decisions in the long run. The mind stays open to think through broader perspectives and possibilities. We have better control of our attention and the effectiveness of working memory. The abundance mindset helps us identify connections and consider the unknown.

- Developing an abundance mindset takes ongoing awareness. Replacing thoughts of scarcity begins with beliefs and understanding what they mean. If you follow your thoughts and see where they lead, be open to what you observe. You will surface patterns and themes. In your organization, you will discover scarcity in how you work and what you produce. You will notice the scarcity mindset in decision-making processes and managing performance. The best way to evolve scarcity thinking is by shifting the collective mindset to abundance.

- Spotting scarcity thinking in conversations provides an opportunity to reframe beliefs. By making beliefs visible, we can identify the assumptions. People's perception of a lack of resources often comes up. When it does, question the perspectives and approach to achieve outcomes. Look for opportunities to reframe scarcity thoughts to abundance when discussing risks, potential, and new opportunities in the organization.

- The scarcity mindset manifests in closed, linear, and transactional business models. The 21st century needs the opposite to meet challenges and create a better future. The concept of regeneration offers a way to innovate and transform. Regeneration represents a continuous cycle of creation, growth, and restoration. Regeneration practices focus on renewing and creating sustainable systems that extend life. Developing new systems and methods provides opportunities to do what hasn't been done before. Shifting the mindset from linear to circular provides perspectives and insights to redesign what we do.

Leading Conscious Transformation

Once you've mastered the five steps of becoming a conscious leader, it's time to begin transforming your organization. And that's a tall order—major change is really hard. Biases set in to influence behaviour to stay close to the status quo. Companies fall into a pattern of doing what they already do, and underlying beliefs and assumptions go unchallenged. Too often, leaders justify their inaction, reasoning that there's not enough time, it's too costly, it's too much change too quickly.

The fallback plan tends to be to adopt new technologies—but the end result is simply the digitization of existing activities. That's not transformational change. The Oxford Dictionary defines transformation as "a thorough or dramatic change in form or appearance." It's the experience of moving from one state to another, a process of metamorphosis. So how do you make it happen for your organization? True transformation is about people, and shifting mindsets to create readiness for the future. That includes building a conscious culture, using conscious innovation, and diving into immersive experiences. This chapter covers all of that.

It's time to rethink how we create transformational change and to understand that it comes from true innovation. To make ground-breaking change, we have to evolve what we do and adjust our internal state. Change has the potential to shift our thoughts, behaviours, and actions; it enables us to function in brand-new ways. To lead change, you must be ready to let go of the old and create the new. Succeeding at transformation is recognizing what's needed for the organization, and making choices that aim to benefit all.

The transformation path is a continuous process. If you see it that way, you'll understand that everyone in your organization has a role to play. It's not the job of one group in your company to run a transformation program, or to rely on a few star players. Rather, you need to embed the transformation experience into how you work so that you evolve together as an organization.

To get started on the transformation path, the first step is to **create readiness**. You have to understand the *why* behind your transformation. The next step is to **envision the future**—this is when you set the intention and develop a clear goal. After that you move into the implementation stage and **design conscious innovation.** To bring that to life, you must **enact immersive experiences**. Finally, to reinforce new beliefs and behaviours, you **build a conscious culture**.

> Create readiness.
> Envision the future.
> Design conscious innovation.
> Enact immersive experiences.
> Build a conscious culture.

CREATE READINESS

The reasons behind your organization's transformation should be clear to everyone because the consciousness you bring to the process determines the outcomes. Without clarity, you'll lack awareness of what you're creating, and the thoughts, feelings, and intentions that influence your actions will stay hidden away. So, it's imperative to establish this understanding in your organization. It starts with having transparent conversations at the top of the organization. Successful leaders know that they must experience first-hand what needs to change, and why, so they can develop deep awareness that informs how best to navigate transformation.

In 2013, Andy Byford was hired by the Toronto Transit Commission (TTC) to overhaul and modernize the system. As Canada's largest transit agency, and the third largest in North America, the TTC desperately needed a total transformation. It was outdated, had significant operational issues that angered and confused passengers, and was stuck in the past. Having just successfully led the transformation of the London Underground system, Byford, as CEO of the TTC, set off on a five-year plan. He knew that part of this transformation was getting back to basics by putting the customer first. Byford called his plan a sea change in how the TTC is run and interacts with employees, customers, and stakeholders. The vision was simple: "A transit system that makes Toronto proud." Byford, along with TTC executives, met with all 12,500 staff over the course of few weeks to discuss the vision. They wanted to ensure that employees understood and bought into the change required to modernize the TTC.

Communication of the "why" behind transformation goes beyond one-time or periodic activities. The conversation needs to become real, and part of how you work, not a one-time session that you hold at the very start. It's helpful to remember that you're speaking *with* people and not *at* them.

After bringing his five-year plan to life for the TTC, Byford was lured by New York City Transit to do the same job for that city. (There, he became a beloved figure known as "Train Daddy.") Amtrak has since hired him to lead its transformation. What's the key to Byford's success as a transformation leader? He is acutely aware that people are at the centre of any transformation. Yes, he modernized TTC operations and its fleet, introduced a smart-card system, oversaw a new six-station subway expansion, installed new automatic train signals to vastly improve subway efficiency, negotiated four-year contracts with the TTC union—these are major things—but he knew those improvements alone wouldn't be enough to deliver a lasting new vision. Byford oversaw the critical change of TTC employees starting to treat passengers as people and not as cargo, and of TTC managers treating employees with respect. Known as a great communicator, Byford would also speak directly with customers while riding the transit system. The TTC is still not perfect. But Byford did what leaders should do: Observe the experiences of others by talking with those most impacted by change. That gives leaders the clearest insight into how to mobilize transformation.

A sharp focus on evolving an organization's most important capabilities helps drive the greatest change to create the most value. And that comes from envisioning the future and setting clear intention and goals.

"BUT WHY?" HOW TO COMMUNICATE TRANSFORMATION

Developing a communication strategy as part of your approach to enabling readiness and change will go a long way. Notice that I haven't referred to this process as "change management." Many change methodologies take root from theory developed in the 1970s. I don't think these old philosophies make sense in today's world. You don't manage change; you enable it by flowing with it. If you manage it, you're resisting it. Change is dynamic, and communication is a significant component in supporting your employees through the transformation experience.

Set the Stage

Start out with an initial communication to your organization in which you share why you're embarking on this path, and why now. Let employees know what to expect. Usually, their immediate concerns are about layoffs. Any information you can share with employees early on can help ease their fears. You should also let employees know how you will continue to communicate with them. When can they expect to hear more? What's the cadence? Like Andy Byford and the TTC executives, hosting town halls and speaking to employees in settings where they can ask questions directly demonstrates openness, transparency, and care. Spending time with people pays off.

Bring It to Life
Set milestones for when key communications will be shared within your organization. It's helpful to plot these out in a calendar. For one, it's an easy way to get all executives on the same page of what to communicate and when. Second, you have clarity of how the story will unfold in your organization, and the way it is building up. You can spot gaps in messages and remedy that more quickly.

Be Open to Adjusting the Plan
Communication will be ongoing, and although you have a plan you're following, be open to adjusting it as you move along. When you provide updates, don't just give a status update—that's boring and not engaging. People will start ignoring it or skimming through information. Keep your communications engaging by sharing what people are learning. Describe what's unfolding in the transformation process. Be open to discussing issues and how you're tackling them. Employees will also learn through what you share. These are important opportunities to build collective knowledge in your organization that will help you to execute.

One More Helpful Tip
Keep messages that you share with customers and other stakeholders in a centralized location that employees can

access, such as your intranet or employee collaboration site like Microsoft Teams. That way if they're asked questions by the public, they can respond with confidence, consistency, and clarity.

By clearly and consistently communicating, you're building trust with your people. The exchange of words is currency that you don't want to waste. So be impactful with your words.

ENVISION THE FUTURE

Until 2009, Denmark's largest energy company, Danish Oil and Natural Gas, had a business model of 85/15. That meant 85 percent of its power and heat production was black (oil, gas, and coal) and 15 percent was green (wind). But that year it announced an ambition to flip that business model on its head and aim to become 85 percent green and 15 percent black to help combat climate change. The transition was set to occur over 30 years.

Just three years later, however, it found itself in unexpected trouble: The price of natural gas had fallen by 90 percent, and the S&P downgraded the company's credit rating to negative. The company was in a deep financial crisis, and so they brought in Henrik Poulsen as the new CEO. He looked at the situation as an opportunity for radical transformation, and recognized the need to build a new company with a new future.

What came next was a profound decision to change the core of the organization. A new business and lifeline for sustainable growth would drive accelerated change: Under Poulsen's leadership it set a new goal of completing its transition to 85 percent green energy much more quickly than thirty years. Poulsen understood that making this pivotal change meant paying attention to short-term and long-term needs, and he did the hard thing of evaluating its 12 lines of business, determining that divesting eight of them was the right choice.

One key step along the transformation path was changing the company name to Ørsted, after a scientist who discovered the principles of electromagnetism, to inspire connection to the new purpose. These big moves enabled actions to move from oil, gas, and coal and instead pursue offshore wind power by building new ocean-based wind farms.

Green energy is expected to reach 99 percent of the company's output as soon as 2025. Ørsted achieved great success from its aspiration to be one of the catalysts for systemic change to a greener society. This belief, with a clear vision and goal, enabled it to become world's largest offshore wind company, with a 30 percent share of the global market.

Attaining this kind of ambitious transformation is no easy feat. But the remarkable power of envisioning a future that inspires people helps an organization get through difficult changes. The connection to the future makes change less scary.

There's no point in proceeding with transformation plans without a compelling vision. Once you have this clarity, you believe it, you talk about it with employees, and then you become it through intention.

DESIGN CONSCIOUS INNOVATION

Leaders often use innovation methods that focus on the question, "What problem are we solving?" It's normal in business to think about a problem and then devise a solution. This thought process—"If we can come up with something new, maybe we'll have first-mover advantage to capture market share"—is repetitive and overdone. And your competitors are doing the same thing. Certainly, thinking about a problem can inspire ideas, but focusing on being first to launch an innovation is short-sighted. Leaders limit themselves to solving for that specific problem, fixated on the idea that helping their teams deliver something quickly to market is better than delivering nothing at all. But this can result in wasteful efforts that don't achieve true transformation.

Conscious innovation goes further by focusing on how to create value. It's when you consider innovation as the tool to realizing your organization's true potential. This new perspective influences your employees to work in a design space to uncover transformative solutions with a long-term outlook. That's what drives greater value creation.

The National Women's Soccer League (NWSL) in the United States is doing just that. Led by commissioner Jessica Berman, the NWSL has landed on *Fast Company's* World's 50 Most Innovative Companies of 2024 because it drives innovation and transformation that not only elevates women's soccer, but women's sports as a whole. It's been growing the league and increasing the value of its teams. In only two years, the size of the NWSL office has tripled, and whereas franchises used to sell for between US $2 million and $5 million, one team recently sold for a record $120 million. The league has secured sponsorship deals with Amazon and Nike.

How has NWSL achieved these unprecedented results? Via a relentless pursuit to think differently. It has to because women's pro sports do not have the same resources as men's. The league has had to think about the entire ecosystem and how decisions impact the wider sports landscape. They understand they need to involve many stakeholders in order to make decisions that lead to the best outcomes. For example, they brought together medical and coaching staff, as well as other experts, to assess the well-being of players on a daily basis because maximizing athletes' performance means they'll give fans the best sporting experience. The league also recognizes that to achieve the highest standard on the field and make matches more exciting and competitive, it has to attract the best players, so it doubled its salary cap during 2023 and 2024. This has led to more sold-out stadiums.

The value that the NWSL is generating through its innovation approach shapes a promising, inclusive future for women's professional sports, and not just in the United States. It has raised the bar for women's sports globally. NWSL made a conscious transformation that benefits many, not just one organization.

> **NEEDS-DRIVEN THINKING**
>
> In order to discover ways to innovate, you have to uncover a need, in your market and beyond, and work to meet it. When you consciously think about making that innovation, it's best to detach yourself from the current reality because envisioning the future and distilling your intention gives you a line of sight into possibilities. You can use that to home in on concepts that become innovations you want to develop.

While considering a vision and future intention, the mind can easily fall into constraints: thoughts about costs, how much time the innovation will take, and whether you have the right talent. Instead, focus your attention on what could be possible—that will help you to unearth new innovations. Imagine you're in the future and observing what's happening around you, in your organization, and how you interact with your customers and other stakeholders. To prompt your thinking, consider the following:

- How has the ecosystem evolved, including for your stakeholders? Have your stakeholders changed or are there new ones?
- What is it like to function in a climate-forward, near net-zero or net-zero society?
- How must you operate to be adaptable in an environment that keeps changing?
- What does resilience look like in your organization? How about your ability to move with disruptions in markets, the economy, politics, and the climate?

Working through these questions encourages taking a big-picture view that considers interconnectivity. Keep any insights that emerge top of mind when you discuss ideas. Consider the needs that your organization could meet in a revolutionary way. Ask yourself:

- Are you serving the same customers or new ones?
- Are you in a new market segment, the same, or a hybrid?
- Are you creating value across stakeholders?

> You can assess the ideas that surface against your vision and the future intention. And then you'll have a clearer idea of whether you'll reach your aspiration. During this experience, remember to keep track of your assumptions and whether you find new beliefs or change your existing ones.

Charles Schwab has built its success on a foundation of conscious innovation. The company disrupted the financial services industry by offering low-cost online trading services to individual investors. It created a financial revolution by democratizing access to investment services. Founder Charles Schwab believed that leaders must be innovative and focus on customers. So he constantly looked for ways to improve the business and provide value to them. For 50 years, the company has kept the same focus on a singular mission: to help individual investors take ownership of their financial lives.

This mission has been at the centre of its innovations. In fact, innovation is *everyone's* job. It doesn't matter what role someone has in the organization. Charles Schwab employees are encouraged to come up with solutions by asking questions and not getting constrained by the status quo. The company has a formalized strategy to gather feedback and drive innovation across the organization, holding town halls, discussions with managers, and team planning sessions. Keeping the ideas flowing is key to its culture, and it wants employees to feel supported in what they put forward.

Conscious innovation becomes an intentional process. Awareness of your mindsets and beliefs helps open the pathways to transformation. Valentino, an Italian high-fashion brand, shifted from "me" to "we," focusing on ethics and sustainability to create a purpose-driven company. The move represents a significant change in its business model. Valentino calls it conscious creation. Long criticized for its use of angora, which animal welfare organizations showed is obtained through cruelty to rabbits, the company announced in 2022 that it would stop using it in their fashions, and also halted the production and sale of furs and Alpaca fleece. Valentino joined Textile Exchange, a global non-profit for climate change action in the fashion and apparel industry. The collaboration will build up their competencies in sustainable materials and techniques. Valentino, awarded by PETA for its action, recognizes that to evolve its business it must know when its products no longer align with its market's values. It's prepared to change, and embrace the experience.

ENACT IMMERSIVE EXPERIENCES

Experiences form the basis of how we perceive and understand reality, so *how* you implement transformation in the day-to-day matters a lot. Some organizations end up with hefty transformation plans involving multiple projects, streams of work, deliverables, milestones, and deadlines. The sheer weight of it bogs people down to the point where they can't imagine what the outcomes will look like. So they rely on guesswork, and interactions among teams can suffer from a lack of common clarity. It's much better to make your organization's transformation an immersive experience for everyone.

Immersive experiences encourage people to use their mind, heart, intuition, and body. You're engaging employees' perception and attention in real time to work toward a future goal. Storytelling, prototyping, and simulations bring your transformation to life. These experiences help employees to visualize, sense, and feel what you want to achieve in an alternate reality.

Storytelling

Narratives inside the organization help employees relate to your future by creating an emotional connection. Stories help people understand what to expect and visualize the outcomes you want to create.

Humanity has a long history of learning through storytelling. The brain has an affinity toward stories and, when engaged in one, can push aside mental clutter. A Danish study found that when we listen to a story with emotional intensity, the brain regions that process emotions light up. Researchers at Princeton University discovered that the brainwaves of the storyteller and the listener synchronize. A woman shared a story about going to her prom. The researchers recorded the brain responses of the woman telling the story and of those listening. They wanted to gauge the listeners' comprehension and found that the listeners' brain activity mirrored the speaker's. This sounds mystical, but it isn't. When there's good communication between people, the listener's brain activity starts resembling the speaker's brain activity. So using storytelling as a tool can help your employees establish common understanding that, in turn, helps them to communicate and collaborate more effectively. A shared story means shared understanding.

Nike's masterful storytelling takes root in the iconic campaign launched in 1988: "Just Do It." The tagline was about inspiration, motivation, and dedication, and it featured stories of athletes who struggled in their journey to attain victory. These stories were about emotions that connected with consumers at a deeper level. Nike also shares "Just Do It" stories internally, showcasing its brand values to inspire innovation. One was about cofounder Bill Bowerman discovering the waffle sole back in the early 1970s, when Nike was still a small company. While having breakfast with his wife, he glanced at the waffle iron and got an idea. He later poured rubber into it, and voila: the outer sole innovation. The waffle iron was a wedding present, and it was now ruined. But the sacrifice meant Nike went on to become a global force.

You can use storytelling to engage your organization in the transformation journey. A compelling narrative that employees relate to forges an emotional connection that helps people work together, look ahead, and think critically. The practice of storytelling brings explicit feelings and intuitive knowledge into teams, and the experiences foster alignment among employees and cohesiveness in how they work.

STARTING WITH INTERNAL STORYTELLING

You have endless options for the types of stories that can support your transformation. The main goal is to open people's heart-centred capacity and thinking via interconnectedness. Immersing in stories allows employees to step into your future reality. The imagery and connections build in people's minds to help them perceive and think in new ways. The stories can contain the mindsets and values that reflect your future state.

Collaborating across your organization in order to develop narratives will help you to incorporate multiple perspectives that will make your stories stronger. An internal communications team can lead the development, collection, and maintenance of the stories. But a cross-functional team involving HR, marketing, and representatives from key business areas creates consistency between internal and external messages, and also diversity of thought.

You can develop either a single story about your vision or a series of stories that express points along your transformation path. Crafting narratives through the perspective of employees, customers, and others encourages empathy and relatability when you're developing solutions. In these stories, focus on the future customer experience, employee experience, and how you will interact with stakeholders.

Consider the following when writing these stories:

- Include characters in the story to showcase actions that share the key messages. The characters could be real customers or employees that consent to sharing their story, or you can create composites.
- Know your audience for the story. A story that speaks to executives could be quite different than one geared toward middle managers or front-line employees.
- Place relevant facts, tools, or resources in your story. These are things you want employees to remember or to access as they do their work.
- Keep stories fresh and relevant. You could tell stories about your future intention, strategic goals, teams

collaborating and overcoming challenges, or individual employees and their experience in the transformation.

Test out your internal channels for telling your stories to determine what works best for your organization. Posting written stories and short video reels on your company intranet is a great place. To ensure employees access them, drive them to a specific spot. (The stories may also have a place on your external website, which your marketing experts can take care of.)

Starting with a story can kick start your transformation meetings, if you have important sessions planned with your board, executives, or other groups.

Prototyping

When you design and build test solutions, you're exploring, discovering, and being intentional about learning so that you can inform your next steps. The simple act of sketching out your idea on a napkin is prototyping; it brings a concept into tangible reality. You can look at what you made and fix it, or scrap it and design again.

When the inventors of Trivial Pursuit wondered over beers if they could invent a board game as good as Scrabble, they came up with the theme of trivia. They sketched out the basic concept in a single evening, coming up with six categories of questions and then visualizing what the board would look like. They doodled several game board designs before settling on a "ship's wheel" with six spokes leading to the centre winner's circle. The playing pieces matched the theme. It went on to become the biggest phenomenon in game history, as dubbed by *Time*.

A significant value add is using the prototype for feedback. Soliciting feedback from teams and stakeholders' increases perspectives and helps you to make better-informed decisions. I mentioned in Step 3: Stay Interconnected that I led a major credit card system transformation. My team prototyped it, starting with diagrams, then flow charts, then digital wireframes, and, eventually, IT development. I asked my team to gather customer feedback about the new digital cardholder experience and the new log-in experience. The team went out and spoke with customers, showing them the new features and log-in process, and then shared the feedback with the entire project team. Some IT team members said hearing the feedback made them feel more connected to the project, knowing it would help customers. For the marketing team, the feedback revealed that the top customer concerns were data privacy and security. The team had assumed the concerns would be about the new features, so they revised the FAQs and other customer resources. The credit card system go-live was a great success. Customers called in to say how much they liked the changes, which was quite a pleasant surprise.

Prototyping is remarkable in that way; developing and testing models produces new knowledge, including that your assumptions about what customers are thinking are wrong. Feedback from it leads to improvements and helps you to check biases. The process of prototyping provides transparency of decisions and where they came from, and it gives more opportunity to use intention and be purposeful. Sharing the lessons across the organization improves everyone's awareness. Being open throughout the experience without attachments encourages a greater connection to deliver better outcomes.

People accept that the work in progress will evolve, and so they're open to change.

Simulations

Playing out scenarios and engaging in practice uncovers insights that flush out assumptions. Like prototyping, it's testing out ideas, but simulating lets you experience actions. The lived experience helps you reflect upon what you went through and then learn from it. You're engaging how you feel and what you think. You can tease out assumptions and perspectives that help you to build solutions that you haven't before. Role-playing is an example of a simple, low-cost way to simulate experiences. You can mock up a new customer experience and act it out to observe the interactions between the customer and employee. You can also use technologies to simulate scenarios for innovations, such as virtual/augmented reality, machine learning, and artificial intelligence.

France-based multinational Schneider Electric has shifted from being purely a hardware supplier to an energy management provider via an open Internet of Things (IoT) platform. It is a global leader, taking the charge to innovate and deliver integrated digital solutions and electrification to create positive climate impact. Its transformation into energy management focused on learning, experimentation, and scaling up its agility. It did not push processes and tools. Instead, Schneider Electric knew that transformation must focus on shaping employee's mindsets and behaviours for innovation, customer-centric solutions, and empowerment—and that establishing these new behaviours would come from experimentation before making changes to its roles, team structure, and operating model. Schneider let its project teams experiment with new agile practices to figure out what works best in specific areas. Employees learned by doing to identify the best practices and scale the right projects in service of their transformation.

Curating these purposeful immersive experiences for employees enables transformation and creates a deeper familiarity with the future you're striving to achieve. As teams collaborate, openness to new insights, thoughts, and beliefs inspires even more innovation. Each person's inner growth contributes to the organization as a whole, which leads to the foundation of continuous learning, priming a readiness for the future where your desired outcomes are achieved. Leveraging conscious experiences for the benefit of all makes transformation that much easier to achieve.

BUILD A CONSCIOUS CULTURE

Enabling significant transformation requires paying attention to your organization's culture. In fact, it's your organization's very foundation. When I ask leaders about their company culture, the responses vary. Some speak with confidence about it, listing core values and sharing what they enjoy about their culture. Others don't really give a clear response; they stumble when trying to describe their internal environment or they speak with hesitation.

Once, I was part of a team working on a massive technology transformation in a financial institution. The project had gone all wrong, and we were re-planning it with the customer experience at the centre. Everything was going to change for employees and customers, and because the ways of working would become fundamentally different, I saw it as an opportunity to evolve the corporate culture. But when I brought that up with one of the team leaders, they said, "Culture is too big a topic with too many variables so we need to leave it out of scope." I didn't know what to say. How can culture be out of scope? The project was completed successfully, but aspects of the culture remained unchanged. Implementing change in that organization was difficult. It always required significant effort to set context, repeat and reinforce messages, and find creative ways to get through resistance. Unfortunately, I think it's still one of its detriments.

Leaders who are apprehensive about culture lack understanding or experience in dealing with it. But even leaders who feel comfortable in the space must make an effort to keep culture in sight. Those at the top of an organization have a prominent role to play in promoting a culture that aligns with their values, mission, and vision for the future. Charles Schwab has a culture of innovation, focusing on the future, and putting the client at the centre of everything they do. That came from the founder, Charles Schwab himself, and continues today.

Organizations with a culture of defined values fare better when undergoing major changes. The clarity helps establish expectations for behaviours. Values that link to how you want people to show up encourage aligned actions. For instance, if transparency is one of your values, you can describe how to demonstrate it. You could identify scenarios of how to communicate with transparency. Internally, that might mean you make it a practice to share decision criteria. With stakeholders, you might decide it's important to communicate frequently and get feedback. The organization's values, behaviours, and corresponding actions contribute to cultural norms.

Patagonia, the outdoor apparel company valued at some US $3 billion, reflects its culture in everything that it does. It engages transparently with employees and stakeholders, an approach it calls "Do the right thing." In a bold move in 2022, Patagonia named Earth as its only shareholder and changed its ownership structure to channel profits it doesn't need to reinvest into protecting nature and fighting climate change. Founder Yvon Chouinard wanted the organization to be an "uncompany," and culture was leveraged to build performance and purpose.

Employees are a critical part of demonstrating the organization's values. Patagonia wants employees to bring new perspectives from previous experiences and their passions. So managers read resumés from the bottom up, seeking out what they dub "dirtbags"—people who love the outdoors. It's important to the company to hire employees inspired by its mission "to save our home planet." Just as strong is Patagonia's culture of helping employees. If employees need help in their personal lives, the People Department is there for them. The company also invites ideas and feedback, and really listens to employees. That's also how they find the most innovative ideas.

The cultural atmosphere of an organization either enhances or erodes how people feel about their jobs; it enters the conscious and unconscious minds of employees, influencing how they perceive, feel, and behave. Leaders, beware: Employees do notice it when what you say is different from the reality of the workplace they experience so consistent behaviour is important. Words about your culture should match the experience.

> **UNDERSTANDING YOUR CULTURE**
>
> Don't be afraid of your organization's culture or see it as a black box of the unknown. In order to shift your culture so that it aligns and accelerates your transformation, you should know what's there. Understanding your corporate culture requires observation with an open mind. If you feel confident about what your culture is, that's great. But there's always opportunity to evolve it and create the best synergy with your transformation path—especially if you're planning major pivots of your business model.
>
> When you bring awareness to the forces at play in your culture, anything can happen. You will need to have senior leaders and other levels of management on board. It's important to set the stage of why you want to unearth what's in your culture and what that will lead to. The expectations should also be set for transparency, accountability, and taking actions to make the appropriate shifts. Consider the following elements of your culture:
>
> - **Shared values:** Are core brand values transparent during strategic, complex, and high-risk decision-making?
> - **Unconscious bias:** Can you spot this in talent management and stakeholder relations?
> - **Behaviours:** Are expectations defined for behaviours in internal, external, individual, and team situations?

- **Decision-making:** Is there clarity of decision-making processes organization wide and at various levels?
- **Collaboration:** What is the nature of internal collaboration across departments, teams, and people—and does it match what's required for your transformation? What about with stakeholders and the ecosystem?
- **Innovation:** Do you have defined innovation processes and practices that employees are aware of? Do any of the innovations end up being delivered and brought to market?
- **Alignment:** Are there gaps in your organization's vision, strategy, goals, intention, and initiatives/projects? Does the flow of work from front-line employees to executives support quick identification and resolution of issues?
- **Recognition:** How and when are employees acknowledged for their contributions? Is recognition given to contributions that match your future vision?

After looking into these dimensions of your culture, you will discover what's helping your organization and what's slowing down performance. Your HR team can provide data about roles, behavioural expectations, decision authorities, and recognition. Canvassing your middle manager, and those above them, for insights about collaboration will give you the best picture of what truly happens. Remember: A conscious culture brings together your values and beliefs, and that will continuously influence people's behaviour and actions.

Your employees are at the centre of the change, and the more you understand it, the greater your capacity will be to shift it. Leaders need to notice and sense what's happening or they can miss warning signs. The symptoms show up in low engagement, poor innovation, slow progress, and lacklustre performance.

Learn to tune into your company's culture. Every conversation and experience opens the capacity for change so it's worth the effort to focus on how people work. If you do, you'll have a greater connection with your company's stakeholders. You'll become more adept at finding innovation and new opportunities.

Take Wolt, a technology company in Finland that has used a conscious culture to innovate. Wolt, whose mission is to make cities better for customers, merchants, and couriers, started out in the Scandinavian Peninsula, a tough market that's both small and spread out. To figure out food delivery, it had to do things differently. So as it expanded, Wolt's leadership built a company culture based on ownership, working efficiently, staying humble, and collaborating. It empowered employees to make decisions, and avoided the rigid hierarchies that dampen innovation and slow progress. At Wolt, product teams have complete ownership of what they build and how. It's their job to understand customer needs. This has created a culture that is innovative and has strong accountability. That's a recipe for success. Just one decade after it launched in 2014, Wolt has expanded from Finland to 25 countries and is now an industry leader. It has joined forces with U.S.-based DoorDash to connect restaurants, retailers, couriers, and customers. The company also operates its own branded grocery store, Wolt Market.

Leading your organization to develop a conscious culture provides a renewable source of energy to achieve your transformation. You move away from taxing people's cognitive capacities to helping them grow—and that means your organization does, too.

> **KEY TAKEAWAYS**
>
> - Many corporate transformation strategies fall short of innovation. Companies keep doing what they always have, and the underlying beliefs and assumptions go unchallenged. Transformation is moving from one state to another in a process of metamorphosis. Thus, transformation is an experience, and we must understand it that way.
>
> - The first step of the transformation path is creating readiness, and the next steps are envisioning the future, setting the intention, and developing a clear goal. After that you're in implementation, designing conscious innovation and delivering it through immersive experiences. New beliefs and behaviours are reinforced through establishing a conscious culture.
>
> - The most critical aspect of transformation is understanding the thoughts behind it. The beliefs about your organization's transformation should be clear to everyone—especially the *why*. These perspectives shape the outlook of employees and actions. Residing at the heart of it are shifting mindsets, increasing awareness, and new thinking. Communication about

the *why* is continuous and should become part of how you work.

- Establish a compelling vision, set your future intention and goals, then proceed with conscious innovation. Leaders considering transformation often think about the problem to solve. Instead, you need to bring your attention to how to create value. Conscious innovation requires a clear understanding of what you bring into designing transformation. To succeed in becoming an innovative company, you need to develop innovation as a strategic capability that all participate in.

- Immersive experiences create shared journeys that connect employees in people-centred environments that focus on learning. Experiences like storytelling, prototyping, and simulations bring you into the transformation. Setting up your organization for success harnesses awareness and attention in these experiences. These experiences help employees to visualize, sense, and feel what you want to achieve in an alternate reality—the future you desire to create.

- Storytelling uses narratives internally that help employees relate to your future by creating an emotional connection. Stories enable people to understand what to expect and help them to visualize the outcomes you want to create. Prototyping is conceptualizing, designing, and building test solutions. You can identify improvement and risks, and seek out feedback from stakeholders. In simulations, acting out scenarios and practising uncovers insights that help identify assumptions and new perspectives.

- Enabling significant transformation requires paying attention to your organization's culture. The critical elements of culture that need attention include implicit and explicit beliefs. These beliefs influence the daily experiences of employees. Whatever is in the culture enters the conscious and unconscious minds of people. The influence reaches perceptions, feelings, and behaviour. To use culture as a catalyst for transformation, you need to know what it consists of.

- Creating a conscious culture takes alignment with your transformation path, and embodies the mindsets and behaviours of future intention. Conscious culture knits together values, beliefs, mindsets, behaviours, and actions. The evolution of it comes from awareness of experiences and creating new ones with intent.

Conclusion

Meeting the challenges of leading a business in this century must come from new thinking and awareness. The ways of the past will not get us to the future. If we don't begin to lead with a new kind of consciousness, those old ways will perpetuate despite our new external environment. For one thing, the technological evolution is already changing the world as we know it. Leaders must prepare for what's ahead through actions in the present. And learning how to lead to a better future requires understanding consciousness—because being attuned to our thoughts, beliefs, and feelings can make us more successful than ever.

Generating this new kind of thinking provides the path to the future. Yet, getting there means we have to eliminate the obstacles in our own minds because the mind, as we've seen, is not that rational.

We are prone to mental errors that result in ineffective decisions. These errors are caused by a number of things, including distractions that take our attention off track and trying to do too many things at once. Cognitive biases, too, affect how we process and interpret information. The brain has its limits, so it attempts to simplify information by using rules of thumb to make sense of the world, but that causes us to make inaccurate and flawed conclusions. Mental models—the ingrained constructs that help us understand conscious experience and how we interact with the world—also play a significant role in how we think. They filter out information and lead to assumptions, which affects how we reason and how we behave.

What can we do about all the traps the mind lays for us? Being aware that the mind can go wrong helps, but it's not enough. We have to understand our whole consciousness. Consciousness extends beyond the brain and comes from awareness of the subjective experience. The heart, gut, and body provide insights that we notice more clearly when we pay attention. Aligning these parts of ourselves in an experience increases awareness. The mind, feelings, and intuition change how we perceive and understand what's happening. The five steps of conscious leadership we covered—be present, become heart-centred, stay interconnected, feel the future, and think with abundance—offer the pathway to a brighter future.

BE PRESENT

Our attention can escape at any moment with little to no effort. Numerous stimuli and distractions constantly bombard us. Coupled with the brain's limitations for capacity, the result is fragile attention. Our mind can begin to wander without us even noticing, and it can go in any direction. We might think about the past or what-ifs that may never occur. This mental chatter takes attention away from the present moment, and when that happens, the conditions for making mistakes and misjudgments are perfect. This is because every time our attention is not in the present, our awareness lowers, and we miss out not only on what's happening around us but also within us. Being present brings awareness to the experience without judgment and expectations. We move into observing the experience instead of getting caught in it, and so we notice more.

Developing habits that strengthen attention and awareness improves sustaining being present. Try this one: When you notice your mind wandering, bring your attention back to your actions. Thoughts that match what you're doing help to sustain focus—plus, it makes you happier. Becoming aware of how you pay attention will enable you to see beneath the tip of the iceberg. And that's a good thing. Seeing reality, and more of it, will steer you away from making critical mistakes that could hurt you and your organization.

BECOME HEART-CENTRED

We live in a world dominated by the mind. We don't learn how to use information from feelings and intuition. But when we lead only with our heads, the ego can come out strong, and that can trigger our brain's fight-or-flight response and other defensive behaviours. Dropping into fear mode erodes the quality of our thinking.

Yet the brain is not the only area with intelligence. The heart and gut have millions of neurons that play a role in cognition and decision-making. The heart can sense, and it can send messages to the brain. The gut can manifest feelings from intuition that turn into sensations in the body. Paying attention to your emotions and intuition creates interoceptive awareness. We learn to understand the insights. But that also comes from distinguishing heart intelligence from mental chatter. Quieting the mind and knowing our normal state of being brings out our inner voice more clearly.

Heart-centred capacities enable perception and better relatability with people and the environment. We develop empathy and compassion, and strengthen relationships. Improving how we perceive ourselves and others changes how we understand the external world. Because when we perceive more and can think through the perspective of others, we tap into new sources to discover opportunities and innovation. Our thinking becomes greater with emotions and intuition. We increase the quality, speed, and accuracy of decision-making.

STAY INTERCONNECTED

We tend to think of ourselves as separate from everyone and everything. This illusion of separateness comes from the ego. Seeing ourselves or our organizations as distinct promotes a mode of thinking that's linear, transactional, and lacks reciprocity. It's us versus them, and when we see the world that way, others around us do, too.

Breaking away from that mental model requires shifting focus to interconnectedness. Interconnectedness directs attention to the external environment. We understand the relationship between the self and the outer world. This kind of thinking enables us to identify the many connections, relationships, and interactions among stakeholders. Establishing an ongoing connection improves our decision-making and the possibility of creating more value.

We can develop a decision-making process that helps us think about stakeholders, the impacts on them, and how to maximize value for all. To discover new opportunities, we should consider ourselves to be part of the ecosystem, and change passive connections to active ones. From the external environment, we will gain perspectives about how to create innovation.

FEEL THE FUTURE

Focusing on the short-term causes us to value today more than the future. That's natural because the brain struggles to think about the far future, preferring predictability and certainty over uncertainty of a goal in the distant future. The way to get around that is to create experiences that allow our senses to immerse in imagining the future. Curating specific experiences can help employees envision and consider alternate realities. We can simulate the future through methods such as prototyping, role-playing, and leveraging digital technology. These experiences provide depth, emotion, and imagery to perceive and create a slice of the future. People gain familiarity and better comprehend what we are trying to achieve.

Setting the future intention connects with what it will *feel* like to reach future outcomes; it guides our actions and reinforces our connection to the actions. Intentions are a state of being that embodies the essence of the future, and they can be set for the company's future, strategic projects, or day-to-day activities. By creating fewer goals and setting intention, it will increase the chances of successful execution. Deep clarity and focus of the future makes it that much easier to take actions on what seems so far away.

THINK WITH ABUNDANCE

The prevailing mindset in many companies is scarcity. The perception of lacking creates a fixation on insufficient resources, which causes feelings of stress and anxiety that distort attention and affect decision-making. Thinking and behaviour gravitate to the short term with less care for long-term value. The scarcity mindset focuses on financial dimensions.

The abundance mindset, on the other hand, is when we see limitless potential. Resources are thought of as enough for everyone. The lens of abundance provides perspective to rethink what we do. We can focus on outcomes even if resources are low, and make better decisions for the long run. Whenever we consider risks, potential, and new opportunities, let's reframe any thoughts of scarcity.

In this century, we need business models that are the opposite of scarcity. Thinking about regeneration offers a new way to innovate and create transformation, and represents a continuous cycle of creation, growth, and restoration. The benefits extend to us as leaders and everyone we interact with in the external environment. Practising abundance involves creating new thought patterns, habits, and behaviours. Replacing thoughts of scarcity with thoughts of abundance helps us to innovate and redesign what we do, and create value beyond the financial dimension.

To become a conscious leader who can guide your organization through these complex and turbulent times, try to master the five steps I've outlined in this book. In this VUCA world (see page xii), paying attention is the greatest resource you have. If you do nothing, you open your organization to great risks. Staying on the path of status quo will make you worse off as time goes on. Becoming a conscious leader will help you to see reality more clearly, and in turn you'll make better decisions with better results. You can avoid the abyss by using your head, your heart, and your gut to perceive and interact with the world around you.

You will equip yourself to lead your organization through conscious transformation. Your recognition of the transformation experience will help you to shift the mindsets of your people to create readiness for the future. You will be able to lead an organization with a conscious culture, one that consciously innovates and learns from immersive experiences. You will steer your people's attention and awareness through the ebbs and flows of the transformation journey. As your organization becomes more conscious, so will the people within it. Everyone's awareness of reality elevates, and that will help you to take action.

This means you as the organization's leader must transform from the inside. You need to recognize the link between your consciousness and creating the future. This will bring about a significant shift in the way you perceive the world and the way you engage with it. Meeting the challenges and opportunities that the 21st century brings is all about how you see a new world. Its potential is significant, but you can create change within yourself and for the people in your organization only by noticing, understanding, and becoming that future. So the path to getting there must differ from the one that has led you to where you are today. Without evolving how you perceive that change, the outer world becomes stagnant. Thoughts become reality.

This century calls for a pivotal change. A new way into the future will come from how you decide to lead. Aligning your mind, heart, body, and intuition in present-moment awareness shifts consciousness. You will see a new path, and a new way of leading and being in this world.

> *It's time for leadership and business to reflect this new kind of consciousness.*
> *That's the only way to a better, brighter future.*

Bibliography

Understanding the Error-Prone Mind

Amos Tversk and Daniel Kahneman. (1974). "Judgment Under Uncertainty: Heuristics and Biases." *Science,* New Series 185 (4157): 1124–31.

D.J. Simons and G.F. Chabris. (1999). "Gorillas in Our Midst: Sustained Inattentional Blindness for Dynamic Events." *Perception.* doi: 10.1068/p281059. PMID: 10694957.

Daniel Jacobs and Lawrence P. Kalbers. (2019). "The Volkswagen Diesel Emissions Scandal and Accountability." *The CPA Journal.* www.cpajournal.com/2019/07/22/9187/

Daniel Kahneman, *Thinking, Fast & Slow.* New York: Penguin.

Derek Lusk. (2020). "The Psychology of Kodak's Downfall." *Psychology Today*. www.psychologytoday.com/ca/blog/unnatural-selection/202008/the-psychology-kodak-s-downfall

Erika Blumenfeld. (2011). "Exposing the Human Side of BP's Oil Spill." *Aljazeera*. www.aljazeera.com/news/2011/5/17/exposing-the-human-side-of-bps-oil-spill#:~:text=Mike%20Robicheux%2C%20a%20doctor%20in,the%20history%20of%20this%20country

Flight International. "Unprofitable PanAm Makes Northwest Bid." (1989). *Flight International*. Archived January 12, 2012, Wayback Machine.

Florida Museum. "Risk of Death." www.floridamuseum.ufl.edu/shark-attacks/odds/compare-risk/death/

Internet Encyclopedia of Philosophy. "Conciousness," Section 2. https://iep.utm.edu/consciousness/#H2

J.F. Kihlstrom. (1987). "The Cognitive Unconscious." *Science* 238: 1445–52.

Jenn Monnier. (2021). "What Was the Deepwater Horizon Disaster." *Live Science*. www.livescience.com/deepwater-horizon-oil-spill-disaster.html

Joe Castaldo. (2016). "The Last Days of Target." *Canadian Business*. www.canadianbusiness.com/the-last-days-of-target-canada/

Justin Gallagher. (2014). "Learning about an Infrequent Event: Evidence from Flood Insurance Take-up in the US." *American Economic Journal: Applied Economics* 6 (3): 206–33.

K.J.W. Craik. (1943). *The Nature of Explanation*. Cambridge: Cambridge University Press; and P.N. Johnson-Laird. (1989). "Mental Models" in M. I. Posner (ed.), *Foundations of Cognitive Science*. Massachusetts: MIT Press, pp. 467–99.

Mark Solms. *The Hidden Spring*. New York: WW Norton, p. 142.

Mengqui Sun and Jack Hagel. (2020). "Volkswagen Tries to Change Workplace Culture That Fueled Emissions Scandal." *The Wall Street Journal*. www.wsj.com/articles/volkswagen-tries-to-change-workplace-culture-that-fueled-emissions-scandal-11601425486

Minda Zetlin. (2019). "Blockbuster Could Have Bought Netflix for $50 Million, but the CEO Thought It Was a Joke." *Inc.com*. www.inc.com/minda-zetlin/netflix-blockbuster-meeting-marc-randolph-reed-hastings-john-antioco.html

National Archives. Vietnam War U.S. Military Fatal Casualty Statistics. www.archives.gov/research/military/vietnam-war/casualty-statistics

National Oceanic and Atmospheric Administration. "Deepwater Horizon Oil Spill Settlements: Where the Money Went." www.noaa.gov/explainers/deepwater-horizon-oil-spill-settlements-where-money-went#:~:text=The%20Deepwater%20Horizon%20criminal%20case,half%20directly%20benefits%20the%20Gulf

National Wildlife Federation. "Deepwater Horizon's Impact on Wildlife." www.nwf.org/oilspill

NRDC. (2015). "Summary of information Concerning the Ecological and Economic Imacts of the BP Deepwater Horizon Oil Spill Disaster." www.nrdc.org/sites/default/files/gulfspill-impacts-summary-IP.pdf

Pragya Agarwal. (2020). "What Neuroimaging Can Tell Us about Our Unconscious Biases." *Scientific American*. www.scientificamerican.com/blog/observations/what-neuroimaging-can-tell-us-about-our-unconscious-biases/

Raymond McDaniel. (n.d.). "The Worst CEOs in American History." *Business Insider*. www.businessinsider.com/the-worst-ceos-in-american-history-2010-5#raymond-w-mcdaniel-jr-14

S. Dekker. (2011). *Drift into Failure: From Hunting Broken Components to Understanding Complex Systems* (1st ed.). Florida: CRC Press. https://doi.org/10.1201/9781315257396

Sidney Dekker. Papers. https://sidneydekker.com/papers/

T. Gilovich and K. Savitsky. (1996, March/April). Like Goes with Like: The Role of Representativeness in Erroneous and Pseudoscientific Beliefs. *The Skeptical Inquirer* 20 (2): 34–30.

United States Environmental Protection Agency. "Deepwater Horizon – BP Gulf of Mexico Oil Spill." www.epa.gov/enforcement/deepwater-horizon-bp-gulf-mexico-oil-spill

Step 1: Be Present

Amishi Jha. (2017). "The Science of Taming the Wandering Mind." *Mindful*. www.mindful.org/taming-the-wandering-mind/

Amishi Jha. (2020). "The Brain Science of Attention and Overwhelm." *Mindful*. www.mindful.org/youre-overwhelmed-and-its-not-your-fault/

B.C. Ministry of Public Safety and Solicitor General, Office of the Superintendent of Motor Vehicles. "Addressing the Problem of Distracted Driving and its Impacts to Road Safety." Discussion paper. www2.gov.bc.ca/assets/gov/driving-and-transportation/driving/roadsafetybc/publications/research-2009-distracted-driver-discussion-paper.pdf

Gisela Telis. (2010). "Multitasking Splits the Brain." *Science Advisor*. www.science.org/content/article/multitasking-splits-brain

J.C. Stutts, D.W. Reinfurt, L. Staplin, and E.A. Rodgman. (2001). "The Role of Driver Distraction in Traffic Crashes." Report prepared for AAA Foundation for Traffic Safety. Washington, D.C.

Jo Gunston. (2022). "Lindsey Vonn: I've been through quite a bit in my career, so I understand what grit is." Olympics.com. https://olympics.com/en/news/lindsey-vonn-alpine-skier-grit-success-interview

K. Michelle et al. (2015). "Contemplating Mindfulness at Work: An Integrative Review." School of Business Faculty Publications, 6.

Katrina Malmqvist, personal interview, October 13, 2023.

Matea Saule, personal interview, October 31, 2022.

Matthew A. Killingsworth and Daniel T. Gilbert. (2010). "A Wandering Mind Is an Unhappy Mind." *Science* (330): 932–32. DOI:10.1126/science.1192439

Mihaly Csikszentmihalyi. (2004). "Flow: The Secret to Happiness." TED. www.ted.com/talks/mihaly_csikszentmihalyi_flow_the_secret_to_happiness/discussion?subtitle=en

S. Silcoff, J. McNish, and S. Ladurantaye. (2013). "How Blackberry Blew It." *The Globe and Mail.* www.theglobeandmail.com/report-on-business/the-inside-story-of-why-blackberry-is-failing/article14563602/www.theglobeandmail.com/report-on-business/the-inside-story-of-why-blackberry-is-failing/article14563602/

Steve Bradt. (2010). "Wandering Mind Not a Happy Mind." The Harvard Gazette. https://news.harvard.edu/gazette/story/2010/11/wandering-mind-not-a-happy-mind/

The Talks. (n.d.). "Lindsey Vonn: "Mind Over Matter." https://the-talks.com/interview/lindsey-vonn/

Step 2: Become Heart-Centred

Brandvoice. (2020). "Leadership Lessons from Walt Disney: Perfecting the Customer Experience." *Forbes*. www.forbes.com/sites/disneyinstitute/2020/02/04/leadership-lessons-from-walt-disney-perfecting-the-customer-experience/

C. Donkin. (2016). "Measuring intuition: Nonconscious Emotional Information Boosts Decision Accuracy and Confidence." *Psychological Science*. https://journals.sagepub.com/doi/abs/10.1177/0956797616629403

Christina F. Chick et al. (2020). "My Body, Your Emotions: Viscerosomatic Modulation of Facial Expression Discrimination." *Biological Psychology* (149): 107779. https://doi.org/10.1016/j.biopsycho.2019.107779

D. Axe and M. Gault. (2017). "How U.S. Marines Are Using 'ESP' to Weaponize Intuition." *Daily Beast*. www.thedailybeast.com/how-us-marines-are-using-esp-to-weaponize-intuition/

D. Brooks. (2023). *How to Know a Person: The Art of Seeing Others Deeply and Being Deeply Seen*. New York: Random House.

Eliza Haverstock. (2021). "'I Feel The Divine Feminine Rising': Spanx Founder Sara Blakely on How Intuition Led to Her $1.2 Billion Blackstone Exit." *Forbes*. www.forbesmiddleeast.com/billionaires/world-billionaires/i-feel-the-divine-feminine-rising-spanx-founder-sara-blakely-on-how-intuition-led-to-her-%2412-billion-blackstone-exit

Eric Beidel. (2014). "More Than a Feeling: ONR Investigates 'Spidey Sense' for Sailors and Marines." Office of Naval Research. https://www.onr.navy.mil/media-center/news-releases/more-feeling-onr-investigates-spidey-sense-sailors-and-marines

G. Olya. (2022). "Spanx Founder Sara Blakely Reflects on Her 'Unusual' Business Journey, the Power of Intuition and the Importance of Paying It Forward." *Yahoo! Finance.* https://finance.yahoo.com/news/spanx-founder-sara-blakely-reflects-175149272.html#:~:text="The%20best%20way%20that%20I,the%20right%20time%20for%20me

Grant Soosalu, Suzanne Henwood, and Arun Deo. (2019). "Head, Heart, and Gut in Decision Making: Development of a Multiple Brain Preference Questionnaire." *Sage Journals.* https://journals.sagepub.com/doi/full/10.1177/2158244019837439

J. Andrew Armour. (2007). "The Little Brain on the Heart." *Cleveland Clinic Journal of Medicine* (74):1. www.ccjm.org/content/ccjom/74/2_suppl_1/S48.full.pdf

J. Sonnenfeld. (n.d.). "Herb Kelleher Didn't Have to Be Boring to Succeed." *Chief Executive.* https://chiefexecutive.net/herb-kelleher-didnt-have-to-be-boring-to-succeed/

Jill Stoneberg, personal interview, October 19, 2023.

Käisu Malkki and Asta Raami. (2022). "Transformative learning to solve the impossible: Edge emotions and intuition in expanding the limitations of our rational abilities." In E. Kostara, A. Gavrielatos, and D. Loads (Eds.), *Transformative Learning Theory and Praxis: New Perspectives and Possibilities* (1 ed.). New York: Routledge. https://doi.org/10.4324/9780429450600-7

M.B. Liester. (2020). "Personality Changes Following Heart Transplantation: The Role of Cellular Memory." *Medical Hypotheses,* 135. doi: 10.1016/j.mehy.2019.109468.

Patrice Sulton, personal interview, December 6, 2022.

R. McCraty and M. Zayas. (2014). "Intuitive Intelligence, Self-regulation, and Lifting Consciousness." *Global Adv Health Med.* 3(2):56–65. doi:10.7453/gahmj.2014.013

Step 3: Stay Interconnected

Banca Etica. (n.d.) "About Us." Website. www.bancaetica.it/about-us/

Claudia Baerwolff, personal interview, August 29, 2023. Correspondence December 21, 2023.

D.A. Vaughn et al. (2018). "Empathic Neural Responses Predict Group Allegiance." *Front. Hum. Neurosci.* 12:302. doi: 10.3389/fnhum.2018.00302

E.H. Erikson. (1968). *Identity, Youth and Crisis.* New York: W.W. Norton & Company, Inc.

Environmental Working Group. (2022). "California Officials Confirm PG&E Responsible for Devastating Dixie Fire." Press release. https://www.ewg.org/news-insights/news-release/2022/01/california-officials-confirm-pge-responsible-devastating-dixie

Joshua Bates, personal interview, September 8, 2023.

M. Friedman. (1970). "The Social Responsibility of Business Is to Increase Its Profits." *New York Times Magazine*, 32–33, 122–24.

Nestlé. (n.d.). "Stakeholder Engagement to Create Shared Value." Website. www.nestle.com/sustainability/responsible-business/stakeholder-engagement

R. Sisodia, D. Wolfe, and J. Sheth. (2014). *Firms of Endearment: How World-Class Companies Profit from Passion and Purpose.* New York: Pearson FT Press.

S. Sy and K. Cuevas. (2022). "Many Californians Still 'Trapped' Years After PG&E Fires. Has the Company Improved Safety?" *PBS News.* www.pbs.org/newshour/show/many-californians-still-trapped-years-after-pge-fires-has-the-company-improved-safety

Step 4: Feel the Future

Achim Peters, Bruce S. McEwen, and Karl Friston. (2017). "Uncertainty and Stress: Why It Causes Diseases and How It Is Mastered By the Brain." *Progress in Neurobiology*. doi: 10.1016/j.pneurobio.2017.05.004

Amazon staff. (2024). "Amazon Drones Can Now Fly Farther and Deliver to More Customers Following FAA Approval." Aboutamazon.com. www.aboutamazon.com/news/transportation/amazon-drone-prime-air-expanded-delivery-faa-approval

C. Isidore. (2018). "Decades of Bad Decisions Doomed Sears." *CNN Business*. www.cnn.com/2018/10/16/business/sears-amazon-cause-of-problems/index.html

D. Kahneman. (2011). *Thinking Fast and Slow*. New York: Farrar, Straus and Giroux.

Daniel L. Schacter, Donna Rose Addis, and Randy L. Buckner. (2007). "Remembering the Past to Imagine the Future: The Prospective Brain." *Nature Reviews Neuroscience*. doi: 10.1038/nrn2213

E. Pronin, C.Y. Olivola, and K.A. Kennedy. (2008). "Doing Unto Future Selves As You Would Do Unto Others: Psychological Distance and Decision Making." *Pers Soc Psychol Bull*. 34(2):224–36. doi: 10.1177/0146167207310023

Emily Chung. (2015). "Amazon Tests Delivery Drones at a Secret Site in Canada—Here's Why." *CBC News*. www.cbc.ca/news/science/amazon-tests-delivery-drones-at-a-secret-site-in-canada-here-s-why-1.3015425

Honeywell. (2023). "Honeywell to Realign Portfolio to Three Powerful Megatrends: Automation, Future of Aviation, and Energy Transition." Press release. https://honeywell.gcs-web.com/news-releases/news-release-details/honeywell-realign-portfolio-three-powerful-megatrends-automation

John-Dylan Haynes. (2007). "Revealing Secret Intentions in the Brain." Max-Planck-Gesellschaft. www.mpg.de/550068/pressRelease20070206

Johnson Space Center Office of Communications. (2024). "First Mars Crew Completes Yearlong Simulated Red Planet NASA Mission." www.nasa.gov/missions/analog-field-testing/chapea/first-mars-crew-completes-yearlong-simulated-red-planet-nasa-mission/

Julie Beck. (2017). "Imagining the Future Is Just Another Form of Memory." *The Atlantic*. www.theatlantic.com/science/archive/2017/10/imagining-the-future-is-just-another-form-of-memory/542832/

K. Szpunar et al. (2013). "Memories of the Future: New Insights into the Adaptive Value of Episodic Memory." *Frontiers in Behavioral Neuroscience* 7:47.

Krista J. Munroe-Chandler and Michelle D. Guerrero. (2017). "Psychological Imagery in Sport and Performance." *Psychology*. https://oxfordre.com/psychology/display/10.1093/acrefore/9780190236557.001.0001/acrefore-9780190236557-e-228#acrefore-9780190236557-e-228-div1-5

M. Carmichael. (2023). "Americans Are Noticing Shrinkflation, And They're Not Happy." *Ipsos*. www.ipsos.com/en-us/americans-are-noticing-shrinkflation-and-theyre-not-happy

Mejuri.com. "About Us." Website. https://mejuri.com/ca/en/company/about-us#our-people

S. Harris. (2024). "Many Canadians Are Fed Up with Shrinkflation. So What's Being Done About It?" *CBC News.* www.cbc.ca/amp/1.7114612

S. Patrick Viguerie, Ned Calder, and Brian Hindo. (2021). "2021 Corporate Longevity Forecast." *Innosight.* www.innosight.com/insight/creative-destruction/

Sam Shead. (2017). "One of the Founders of Amazon's Drone Delivery Project Quietly Left the Company and Moved to New York." *Business Insider.* www.businessinsider.com/amazon-prime-air-delivery-drone-founder-daniel-buchmueller-has-left-2017-5

Selfridges & Co. www.selfridges.com/CA/en/reselfridges?cm_sp=MegaMenu-_-ProjectEarth-_-ProjectEarth

Step 5: Think with Abundance

Alter Eco. (2021). "Regeneration Report." www.regeneration2021ae.com

B.L. Hughes and J. Zaki. (2015). "The Neuroscience of Motivated Cognition." *Trends Cogn. Sci.* 19:62–64. doi: 10.1016/j.tics.2014.12.006

Bloomberg. (2023). "Levi's Looks to Cut Denim's Water Impact Where It Most Counts." *Business of Fashion.* www.businessoffashion.com/news/sustainability/levis-looks-to-cut-denims-water-impact-where-it-most-counts/

FAO. (n.d.). "Global Symposium on Soil Erosion." www.fao.org/about/meetings/soil-erosion-symposium/key-messages/en/

Glenn R. Fox et al. (2015). "Neural Correlates of Gratitude." *Frontiers.* www.frontiersin.org/journals/psychology/articles/10.3389/fpsyg.2015.01491/full

Inge Huijsmans et al. (2019). "A Scarcity Mindset Alters Neural Processing Underlying Consumer Decision Making." *PNAS*. doi: 10.1073/pnas.1818572116

Jeff Boss, personal interview, October 13, 2023, and December 15, 2023.

Linda Roszak Burton. (n.d.). "Discovering the Health and Wellness Benefits of Gratitude." Wharton Health Care Management Alumni Association. www.whartonhealthcare.org/discovering_the_health

R. Wiedmer et al. (2020). "Resource Scarcity Perceptions in Supply Chains: The Effect of Buyer Altruism on the Propensity for Collaboration." *Journal of Supply Chain Management* 56(4): 45–64.

Rolan Zahn et al. (2009). "The Neural Basis of Human Social Values: Evidence from Functional MRI." *Cereb Cortex* 19(2): 276–83. doi: 10.1093/cercor/bhn080

S. Mullainathan and E. Shafir, E. (2013). *Scarcity: Why Having Too Little Means So Much.* New York: Times Books.

Thousand Fell. Website. www.thousandfell.com/pages/mission

United Nations. (n.d.). "Water—At The Center of the Climate Crisis." www.un.org/en/climatechange/science/climate-issues/water

Women Together. (n.d.). "Business as a Movement: A Conversation with Eileen Fisher." https://womentogether.com/lifenotes/article/business-movement-conversation-eileen-fisher/

Leading Conscious Transformation

Canadian Encyclopedia. (2024). "Trivial Pursuit." Article. www.thecanadianencyclopedia.ca/en/article/trivial-pursuit

Carolina Valdez. (2023). "Six Things I Enjoy the Most About Working at Wolt." *Wolt Careers*. https://careers.wolt.com/en/blog/tech/what-i-enjoy-about-working-at-wolt

CBC News. (2013). "TTC plans to 'Transform and Modernize' System." *CBC News*. www.cbc.ca/news/canada/toronto/ttc-plans-to-transform-and-modernize-system-1.1351983

CBC Radio. (2022). "How a Waffle Iron Inspired the Nike Shoe." Article. www.cbc.ca/radio/undertheinfluence/how-a-waffle-iron-inspired-the-nike-shoe-1.6482861

Charles Schwab. (2023). "Celebrating 50 Years of Innovation." Article. www.schwab.com/learn/story/celebrating-50-years-innovation

Colin Mitchell. (2002). "Selling the Brand Inside." *Harvard Business Review*. https://hbr.org/2002/01/selling-the-brand-inside

Eric Reguly. (2019). "A Tale of Transformation: The Danish Company That Went From Black to Green Energy." *Corporate Knights*. www.corporateknights.com/clean-technology/black-green-energy/

Fast Company. (2024). "The World's Most Innovative Companies of 2024." www.fastcompany.com/most-innovative-companies/list

Innosight. (2019). "The Transformation 20: The Top Global Companies Leading Strategic Transformations." *Insights*. www.innosight.com/insight/the-transformation-20/

Kate Murphy. (2024). "San Diego Wave Sold for $120M: An NWSL Record." AXIOS. www.axios.com/local/san-diego/2024/03/15/wave-sold-new-owners-nwsl-record

Marcus Gee. (2012). "Andy Byford Gives TTC Energy It Desperately Needed." *The Globe and Mail*. www.theglobeandmail.com/news/toronto/andy-byford-gives-ttc-energy-it-desperately-needed/article4630163/

Mikkel Wallentin et al. (2011). "Amygdala and Heart Rate Variability Responses From Listening to Emotionally Intense Parts of a Story." *Science Direct.* www.sciencedirect.com/science/article/abs/pii/S1053811911007233?via%3Dihub

Muriel Draaisma. (2017). "TTC CEO Andy Byford Stepping Down After 5 Years to Lead New York City Transit." *CBC News.* www.cbc.ca/amp/1.4412120

Patagonia. (2022). "Patagonia's Next Chapter: Earth Is Now Our Only Shareholder." *Patagonia Works.* www.patagoniaworks.com/press/2022/9/14/patagonias-next-chapter-earth-is-now-our-only-shareholder

PETA. (2021). "PETA Fashion Awards." PETA UK. www.peta.org.uk/living/peta-fashion-awards-2021/

Scott D. Anthony, Alasdair Trotter, and Evan I. Schwartz. (2019). "The Top 20 Business Transformations of the Last Decade." *Harvard Business Review.* https://hbr.org/2019/09/the-top-20-business-transformations-of-the-last-decade

Shana Lebowitz. (2019). "Patagonia's HR Chief Says He Reads Resumes 'From The Bottom Up' to Avoid the Culture-Fit Trap." *Business Insider.* www.businessinsider.com/patagonia-hiring-company-culture-add-vs-fit-dean-carter-2019-10

Tarah Wolking. (2021). "Innovating with Intention." *Charles Schwab.* www.aboutschwab.com/mss/story/innovating-with-intention

Uri Hasson. (2010). "Defend Your Research: I Can Make Your Brain Look Like Mine." *Harvard Business Review.* https://hbr.org/2010/12/defend-your-research-i-can-make-your-brain-look-like-mine?registration=success

Valentino. (n.d.). "Valentino Vision: Creating Shared Value." Website. www.valentino.com/en-ca/creating-shared-value?-view=comparableLink&utm_source=newsletter&utm_medium =email&utm_content=creating_shared_value_7th_push&utm_ campaign=x_pres_23#IDpeople

Vinciane Beauchene, Daniel Gheno, and Eric Fournier. (2021). "Lessons from Schneider Electric's Agile-at-Scale Transformation." *BCG*. www.bcg.com/publications/2021/energy-management -company-agile-at-scale-transformation

Index

A

Abby Grind, 9, 10
    abundance mindset
        and decision-making, 134–135
        developing, 151
        and employees, 135
        and gratitude, 138–141
        and leadership, 135–136
        leading with, 143–145
        practising, 150
actor–observer bias, 14
Agile, 35
Alter Eco, 146
Amazon, 114–115
Amazon Prime Air, 114–115
Amtrak, 156
amygdala, 16, 34
"analysis paralysis," 91
Apple, 118
Aristotle, 25
Armour, J. Andrew, 63
assumptions
    and biases, 3, 21
    as cause of mental errors, 20
    and false reality, 7
    how to surface in a meeting, 24
    and mental models, 24, 29
    and normalization of deviance, 7, 8
    normalizing red flags with, 5
    opaque, 21
    versus reality, 3–4, 8
    and scarcity mindset, 145
    shared, 94–95
    suspending, 23
    wrong, 3
    and wrong decisions, 4, 18, 58
attention
    to the body, 52–53
    improving, 45–47, 48–49, 55, 58–59
    as most important leadership skill, 33
    purposeful, 43–45
    signs of waning, 55
    value of, 42–43, 58
attention span, 34–35
attentional capacity, 31–32

B

Baerwolff, Claudia, 97
Banca Etica, 102

Barrett, Lisa Feldman, 74
baseline (normal state of being), 68–71
Bates, Joshua, 103, 104
being present
    challenges of, 32–33, 57
    and envisioning the future, 124, 127
    to improve attention, 45
    and inner state, 52
    and intuition, 73
    as a leader, 53–54
    and mindfulness, 47–48
    and mindset, 138
    versus mind-wandering, 38–39, 58
    in the moment, 39
    at work, 38–39, 41–42
Berkshire Hathaway, 118
Berman, Jessica, 161
Bezos, Jeff, 114
biases
    and assumptions, 3, 21
    awareness of, 17
    and false reality, 7
    how to avoid, 17–18
    and negative emotions, 76
    overconfidence, 66
    personal agenda, 90
    and reality, 3
    transparency around, 17
    unconscious, 15–17, 175
    and wrong decisions, 4
    See also cognitive biases
"black swan" events, 11
Blakely, Sara, 63
Blockbuster Video, 113
Bos, Jeff, 147, 148
Bowerman, Bill, 167
BP, 4, 5, 6–7
brain–gut connection, 65
brand identity, 94
breathwork, 49–51, 142
broadcaster. *See* mental chatter
Brooks, David, 62, 72, 74
Buffet, Warren, 118
Byford, Andy, 155–157

C

Chabris, Christopher, 1
Challenger, 6
Charles Schwab, 164, 173

Chouinard, Yvon, 174
Citizens Bank of Canada, 99
cognitive biases
    actor–observer bias, 14
    confirmation bias, 14
    sunk-cost fallacy, 15
cognitive effort, 12
Cold War, 3
collaboration, 35, 95, 105, 136, 159, 176
collective consciousness, 87
collective thinking, 13
Communism, 3
compassion, 79, 80, 83, 85
Conference of the Parties (COP), 110
confirmation bias, 14
conscious awareness, 16, 28
conscious creation, 165
conscious culture
    building, 154, 172–175, 178–180
    and innovation, 177
    lack of, 172–173
conscious innovation, 160–165
consciousness, 25, 26, 30, 87
corporate culture. *See* conscious culture;
 culture
COVID-19, 11
C-suite disconnect, 97
Cuban Missile Crisis, 3
culture
    of collaboration, 136
    corporate, 173, 175–176, 177
    of defined values, 173
    understanding, 175–176
    See also conscious culture
customers, 78, 164, 170
    See also stakeholder(s)

D

Danish Oil and Natural Gas, 159–160
DC Justice Lab, 82–83
decision-making
    and abundance mindset, 134–135
    and anchoring heuristic, 12, 13
    and baseline state, 69
    bigger-picture, 90–92
    and conscious culture, 176
    by envisioning the future, 122–124
    impaired by stress, 113
    interconnectedness in, 100

and intuition, 62, 63, 65–66, 77–78, 84
outside of yourself, 89–90
over-simplifying, 91
and representative heuristic, 9
rushed, 5, 12, 13
and scarcity mindset, 133, 143, 150–151
slowing down, 18
as tool to expand awareness, 100
Decker, Sidney, 5
Deepwater Horizon, 4–7
default mode network (DMN), 37–38
Descartes, René, 25
Disney, Walt, 67, 78
distracted driving, 36
distracting thoughts, 37–38
distractions
  as cause of mental errors, 29
  examples, 31
  journalling about, 54
  and multitasking, 34
  reducing, 46, 55, 117–118
Door Dash, 177
dopamine, 139
DuBuisson, Jennifer, 137

E

Eileen Fisher, 136
emotional awareness, 13
emotional intelligence, 61
emotional regulation, 73, 76–77
emotions. *See* feelings; heart intelligence; negative emotions
empathy, 79, 80, 83, 85
employees
  and change, 177
  communication with on transformation, 156, 157–158
  connection amongst, 136
  and corporate culture, 173, 174–177, 180
  expressing gratitude for, 139
  immersive experiences for, 166, 172, 179
  putting first, 78
  scarcity mindset amongst, 144
  seeking opinions of, 91
  shared assumptions amongst, 94–95
  and storytelling, 166–169, 179
  and transformational change, 157–158
  using intuition with, 75–76

See also stakeholder(s)
enteric neural plexus, 63
Erikson, Eric, 87–88
ethical banking, 102

F

facial expressions, 67
failure of logic, 2
false reality, 5, 7
false sense of security, 6
fashion industry, 136, 137
feelings, 28, 30, 60–63
  See also heart intelligence
Firms of Endearment: How World-Class Companies Profit from Passion and Purpose (Sisodia et al.), 93
first impressions, 12, 16, 17, 67
focus
  challenge of sustaining, 33
  clearing mental clutter, 13
  importance of, 32
  lack of, 2
  See also attention; being present
Foment Regeneration, 147
Freidman, Milton, 92
future envisioning, 121–129, 154, 159–160
future self, 126–128

G

Gilbert, Daniel T., 39
goals
  how to pursue, 118
  and intentions, 118–120
  reducing, 116–118, 129
gratitude
  and abundance mindset, 138–141
  and journalling, 141–142
  and language, 140
  and mindfulness meditation, 142
  practising, 138–139, 141–143
Great Depression, 19
Green America, 147
"group think," 3–4
Grouse Grind, 9, 10
gut brain, 63, 64–65
gut instinct, 28, 61–62, 65
  See also intuition
gut–brain connection, 65

H

heart brain, 63–64
heart energy, 64
heart intelligence
   in decision-making, 79, 85
   in difficult situations, 80
   experience of, 67–68
   and experiences, 78–79, 80, 85
   and intuition, 66, 75–76
   leveraging, 68–69
   signals, 60–61, 72
   testing, 74–75
   understanding, 74, 84
heuristic(s)
   adjustment and anchoring, 11–12
   availability, 10–11
   avoiding, 13
   awareness of, 13
   mental shortcuts, 8
   representative, 9–10
Honeywell, 112
How to Know a Person (Brooks), 62, 72, 74
human connection, loss of, 35
hypothalamus, 139

I

identity, 87–88
illusion of separateness, 87, 105
immersive experiences, 154
   for employees, 166, 172, 179
   nature of, 165–166
   prototyping, 169–171, 179
   simulations, 171–172
   storytelling, 166–169, 179
Inception (film), 52
individualistic behaviour, 88, 90
inner state awareness, 51–54, 59, 84
inner voice, 72–73, 74, 85, 140
innovation
   conscious, 154, 160–165, 179
   and conscious culture, 176
   culture of, 173
   and future envisioning, 128
   heart-centred, 80–83
   by leaders, 160–161
   and scarcity mindset, 145, 150
   and simulations, 171
   and transformational change, 178
   via needs-driven thinking, 161–164
intentions
   as creating collective experience, 129
   future, 126
   and pursuing goals, 118–120
   setting personal, 120–121
internal dialogue, 39–40, 39–41
Internet of Things (IoT), 171
intrinsic cardiac neural plexus, 63
intuition
   biology of, 63–65
   in decision-making, 65–66, 77–78, 84
   and facial expressions, 67
   and heart intelligence, 73
   inclination to ignore, 61–62
   value of, 62–63
invisible gorilla experiment, 1–2

J

Jobs, Steve, 118
Journal of Management, 48
journalling, 54, 141–142

K

Kahneman, Daniel, 27
Kelleher, Herb, 78
Kennedy, President, 3
Khrushchev, Nikita, 3
Killingsworth, Matthew A., 39
knowledge gathering, 13–14
Kodak, 21–22

L

law of diminishing returns, 18
leadership
   and abundance mindset, 143–145
   and beliefs as value-creation drivers, 94
   bigger-picture decision-making by, 90–92
   disconnect, 97
   heart-centred, 77–80, 82
   and innovation, 160–161
   listening skills of, 91
   mindful, 54–56
   need for consistent behaviour by, 174–175
   role in culture, 173
   and scarcity mindset, 143–146, 151
   skills, typical, 33
   using intuition, 75–76

Levi Strauss & Co., 137–138
limiting thoughts, 140
Lipton, Bruce, 119
"little brains," 63, 84
living in the moment, 39
long-term memory, 26, 26–27
Luskin, Fred, 37

M
Malmqvist, Katrina, 50
Mandela, Nelson, 134
Matea Designs, 53
Max Planck Institute for Human Cognitive and Brain Sciences, 119
McNamara, Robert S., 3, 4
"McNamara's War," 3
meditation
    focused attention, 47–49
    and gratitude, 142
    to improve attention, 48, 59
    modes of practice, 49
    open monitoring, 47–49
Mejuri, 120
mental chatter
    vs. inner voice, 72–73
    nature of, 40
    pros and cons of, 40–41
    reducing, 46–47, 58
mental errors
    assumptions as cause of, 20
    awareness of, 25
    examples, 3–7
    how to avoid, 13–14
    lack of focus, 2
    and multitasking, 29
    shared, 92
    See also heuristic(s)
mental models,
    ability to change, 22
    and assumptions, 20–22, 23, 29
    awareness of, 22–23
    corporate, 95
    explicit, 92, 97
    implicit, 92, 95, 97
    limitations of, 18–20, 22, 29
    role of, 18, 29
    understanding, 22–23
mindfulness, 47–49, 59
    See also meditation

mindfulness meditation. *See* meditation
mindset
    and being present, 138
    shifting, 135, 139, 143–144, 148, 152
    See also abundance mindset; scarcity mindset
mind-wandering, 37–39, 46–47, 58
misconceptions, 4
Mullainathan, Sendhil, 133
multitasking
    avoiding, 36, 55
    as cause of mental errors, 29
    and driving, 36
    with intention, 36–37
    low risk, 37
    and mistakes, 57
    myth of, 34
    and remote work, 35
    task-switching, 34
    and work environments, 35

N
NASA, 122–123
National Airlines, 19
National Women's Soccer League (NWSL), 161–162
needs-driven thinking, 161–164
negative emotions
    avoiding influence of, 76–77
    awareness of chronic, 85
    and inner-state awareness, 53
    and wandering mind, 37
Nest, 112
Nestlé, 101–102
Netflix, 113
New York City Transit, 156
Nike, 166–167
Nolan, Christopher, 52
non-judgmental attitude, 53, 56
normalization of deviance, 6
Northwest Airlines, 19

O
opinions, 91, 105
organization(s)
    communication within, 96, 106
    cultural atmosphere, 174
    culture, 172–173, 180
    decision-making process as tool, 100

as ecosystem, 98–99, 106, 128
explicit mental models, 95, 96, 105
goal setting by, 116–118
identity, 94
implicit mental models, 95–96, 105
leadership disconnect, 97
and scarcity mindset, 151
storytelling, 166
Ørsted, 160
overconfidence, 5
overconfidence bias, 66

P

Pacific Gas & Electric (PG&E), 92
Pan American Airways, 19, 22
Patagonia, 174
perception of reality, 25–28, 30, 80, 85
perception vs. reality, 2, 3
PETA, 165
planning
   far future, challenges of, 114
   future, 111
   with imagination, 115–116
   short-term vs. long-term, 112
   and vision statement, 113
Plato, 25
positive affirmations, 142
Poulsen, Henrik, 159–160
prefrontal cortex, 16
Project Implicit, 17
prototyping, 169–171, 179

R

readiness, creating, 154, 155–157, 178
reality
   vs. assumptions, 3–4
   attention determined by, 56–57
   creation of false, 92
   faulty view of, 19
   future alternate, 165–166, 167, 179
   and mental chatter, 58
   and mental models, 18, 22
   vs. perception, 2–3
   perception of, 25–28, 30, 80, 85
recyclable sneaker, 149
red flags, 5, 8
regenerative business practices, 145–146
regenerative farming, 147–148
regenerative thinking, 147, 152

remote work, 35
Research In Motion, 56–57
risks
   and availability heuristic, 10
   "black swan" events, 11
   and mental models, 18–19
   and normalization of deviance, 6–7
   overlooking, 11
rules of thumb, 29

S

Saule, Matea, 53–54
scarcity mindset
   and fashion, 137–138
   and fear of missing out, 131
   habitual thought patterns creating, 132
   organizations with, 133
   pitfalls of, 133–134, 150–151
   reframing, 140–141, 152
   unawareness of, 132–133
   in workplace, 132
Scarcity: Why Having Too Little Means So Much (Shafir and Mullainathan), 133
Schneider Electric, 171–172
Sears, 113
self-reflection, 138
Selfridges, 111, 148
Senge, Peter, 98
"sensemaking" (situational awareness), 78
sensory perception, 52
separateness, illusion of, 87, 105
Shafir, Eldar, 133
shared mental models, 92, 93
shareholder primacy, 92–93, 94, 105
short-term results, 110
short-term thinking, 109–110
shrinkflation, 109–110
Simons, Daniel, 1
simulations
   future, 122–123, 129
   and innovation, 171
   role playing, 171
   and transformational change, 171–172
Sisodia, Raj, 93
Soil & Climate Initiative, 147–148
Soles4Souls, 149
Solms, Mark, 26
Southwest Airlines, 78, 93
SPANX, 63

stakeholder(s)
　connection with, 81, 83, 93, 99–104, 106–107, 177
　ecosystem, 148
　feedback from, 102, 124–125, 170, 174, 179
　regenerating value for, 147
Starbucks, 93
stereotypes, 16, 17
Stoneberg, Jill, 81
storytelling
　internal, 167–169
　and learning, 167
　Nike, 167–168
　in transformation journey, 167, 179
stress response, 34
subconscious, 16
Sulton, Patrice, 82, 83
sunk-cost fallacy, 15
supply and demand, 18
System 1, 27, 66
System 2, 27
systems thinking, 98
Szpunar, Karl, 114

T

Target, 20–21
Target Canada, 20–21, 22
Teams, 35
Territorial Initiative Groups (TIGs), 102
Textile Exchange, 165
The Biology of Belief (Lipton), 119
The Challenger Launch Decision (Vaughan), 6
The Fifth Discipline (Senge), 98
The Fog of War, 3
The Hidden Spring (Solms), 26
Thinking, Fast and Slow (Kahneman), 27
Thousand Fell, 149
Toronto Transit Commission (TTC), 155–156
transformation, defined, 153–154
transformation path
　build a conscious culture, 154, 172–178
　create readiness, 154, 155–159, 178
　design conscious innovation, 154, 160–165
　enact immersive experiences, 154, 165–172
　envision the future, 154, 159–160
transformational change
　communicating, 157–159
　and employees, 157–158
　innovation as source of, 154
　people-centred, 156
Transocean Ltd., 5, 6–7
Trivial Pursuit, 169

U

unconscious biases, 15–17
UPS, 93

V

vacation trap, 49
Valentino, 164–165
Vancity Community Investment Bank, 99–100, 123, 123–124
Vaughan, Diane, 6
Vietnam War, 3, 4
Virgin Voyages, 80–81, 82
Vonn, Lindsey, 32

W

Whole Foods, 93
Wolt, 177
work environments, 35

X

Xerox, 112–113

About the Author

As a practitioner and steward of conscious leadership, **SEEMA DHANOA** helps leaders to improve their organizations and the planet. With a diverse 20-year career in strategy, execution, and business and technology transformation, Seema has led innovative initiatives within Canada's financial sector and beyond, including the creation of the country's first social impact bank. Drawing from her professional journey and passion for conscious leadership, she authored *The Path to Conscious Leadership*, a practical guide for leaders seeking to create meaningful impact. Today, Seema supports forward-thinking leaders in navigating their own path with purpose, awareness, and empathy. Seema holds a Bachelor of Business Administration from the British Columbia Institute of Technology, and an Executive MBA from the Beedie School of Business at Simon Fraser University.

Originally from Vancouver, B.C., Seema lives in Toronto, Ontario.

www.seemadhanoa.com